A PRACTICAL GUIDE TO TICKETING SUCCESS

All Ticket

Your blueprint for growing attendances, increasing revenue and modernising your football club

David Lynam

Re think

First published in Great Britain in 2025
by Rethink Press (www.rethinkpress.com)

© Copyright David Lynam

All rights reserved. No part of this publication may be reproduced, stored in or introduced into a retrieval system, or transmitted, in any form, or by any means (electronic, mechanical, photocopying, recording or otherwise) without the prior written permission of the publisher.

The right of David Lynam to be identified as the author of this work has been asserted by him in accordance with the Copyright, Designs and Patents Act 1988.

This book is sold subject to the condition that it shall not, by way of trade or otherwise, be lent, resold, hired out, or otherwise circulated without the publisher's prior consent in any form of binding or cover other than that in which it is published and without a similar condition including this condition being imposed on the subsequent purchaser.

Cover image © Shutterstock | Nosyrevy

Contents

Foreword	1
Introduction	5
You're not alone	6
How this book can help	8
1 The Brutal Truth	11
The dungeon	12
Poor ticket sales	14
Not selling tickets online	16
The consequences	18
A much-needed change	24
2 Clarity	27
The importance of planning	28
Controlling experimentation	29
Achieving targets	30
Introducing the five C's	31
Approaching tech in the right way	34
Tracking progress	35

    Looking at the bigger picture   36
    A final word on focus   42

3 Captivate   45
    Solve problems but avoid overwhelm   46
    Tie the action to the problem   50
    Software is not always the answer   52
    Understand the problem from all angles   56

4 Cutting-Edge Tech   63
    The landscape is changing   64
    Ensuring buy-in   67
    Having the right people   69
    What will have the biggest impact?   70
    Technology is a leveller   73
    Tips to get you started   74
    A word on integrations   76

5 Communication   81
    Fan engagement is a thing   83
    Communicating with the fans   86
    Don't forget your international fans   91
    Communicating with overlooked groups   93

6 Confidence   97
    Working on yourself   98
    Working through the season   99
    Don't be a hero   101
    Prepare for Manchester City every week   103

Challenge with confidence	107
Developing the club with the five C's	109
7 Your Ticketing Strategy	**113**
From tactical to strategic	114
It's not just about the club	116
Implications and regulations	118
Let's create	125
8 Fan Experience And Engagement	**129**
It starts with everyone else	130
Technology is an enabler, not the star of the show	132
Fan surveys	135
Reciprocity is key	138
Lucky number seven	142
Partnerships with schools and youth teams	147
First impressions count	149
Get the foundation right	150
9 Revenue Optimisation	**153**
Draw on metrics	155
Become a destination	158
Club memberships	160
You are an international business	164
Think low-cost and think creatively	165
A quick word on virtual tickets	167
Do the best with what you have	170

10 Operational Excellence	173
Get rid of the barriers	176
Community integration and volunteering	177
Training is essential	179
Use historic data to improve match days	183
Operational excellence is everywhere	184
Digital or paper, the choice is yours	187
Conclusion	**191**
What you've learned	192
Going forward	195
Acknowledgements	**199**
The Author	**203**

Foreword

There is a common misconception with people that aren't directly involved in ticketing that it can't be that complicated.

'Doesn't the internet just do it all these days?', and 'you just have to push a button and it's done', and the classic, 'what do you do with your time when the season's over', are among the frequent statements made to me at different times in my career, and probably familiar to many reading this.

However, the reality and complexity are very different. The ticketing operation at any club or venue is so much more than just getting people into the building. It is integral to the entire business, and anyone with any experience in ticketing, will have experienced similar pressures and problems.

It doesn't matter if you are working at a non-league stadium or a state-of-the-art venue with all the bells and whistles. The key demands placed on a ticket office all centre around the similar themes of sales and financial targets, customer service and supporter experience.

In more recent years, these long-standing areas of focus for ticket offices have developed significantly. In addition to the more traditional aspects of ticketing, there is now a strong reliance on technology and data. The move to digital tickets, which was accelerated by the return of fans following the COVID pandemic, has led to a need for additional knowledge and skills in the industry. Educating staff and fans alike puts additional stress on many venues at an already intense time.

However, the move to digital tickets and smartphones as the new ticket, has become an accepted norm at all levels and is a significant change in how many venues now operate. What started as a crucial development that allowed fans to return to stadia and businesses to start recovering some much-needed revenue, soon began to pique interest elsewhere in the industry.

Marketing departments suddenly saw a data capture potential. Safety and security teams began thinking about what data could be gathered to model the behaviour of attendees and allocate staff levels in a more efficient way. As so often is the case, all roads led back to the ticketing team to work through a new wave of requests and requirements from colleagues and governing bodies.

While the last five years has seen a significant change in the traditional processes, just as many things remain the same. Fixture changes, requirements for media obligations and the endless quest to provide internal stakeholders with as much insight into your match going fans as possible means that the biggest skill required to run a solid ticketing operation is still agility.

The ability to solve problems and create solutions quickly and effectively are key necessities in your operation. The moment that you think you have thought of everything, you will be caught out. Always have a backup plan, never rule anything out and build a good network in the industry. If you work for other teams and venues, that in all other aspects are your competitors, they can be an invaluable source of help and support.

If you are reading this book and work in the strange world of ticketing, little of what I have said here will come as a surprise. What you will find in the following pages is some help, a lot of very useful insight, but above all you will get reassurance that you are not alone. The challenges and suggestions that are in the pages to come will resonate and, hopefully, offer some useful ideas to make your world that little bit easier.

ALL TICKET

Having worked with Dave for over twenty years in different roles at The Football Association (FA) and at Tottenham Hotspur, I am delighted to see what he has achieved in the latest phase of his career. Like everyone in any job, we spent many hours discussing the issues we faced, how we would do things better and what changes we would make if we were starting with that fabled 'blank sheet of paper'.

Rather than continue to complain and daydream, he decided to do something about it. Shaped by years of experience and frustrations on the frontline of the industry, Dave took what he's learned from various major events and wrote *All Ticket*, as well as creating his company, Kaizen.

Ian Murphy, Head of Ticketing, Tottenham Hotspur Football Club

Introduction

Managing the ticketing operation at a football club has been a grossly misunderstood and massively underrated skill for far too long. I've used the word 'skill' deliberately there – it is absolutely a skill.

I don't think I've ever met anyone doing this job who left education with the intention of one day becoming a ticket office manager or head of ticketing as a career choice. Instead, we all fell into the wonderful world of selling tickets, one way or another, and haven't been able to escape since. We just happened to be in the right place at the right time and, once there, we never looked back. It's no surprise that people have been doing the job in one way or another for ten, twenty, thirty plus years. It is a black hole. Once you're in, there's no way out and so you just keep going. Like many, you might have a love–hate relationship with the role.

You may also feel misunderstood by most of the people working at your stadium. You possibly suffer from a lack of appreciation from others for the time and effort that goes into what you do. You are a professional problem solver. From the annual jigsaw puzzle of season ticket seat moves to working out segregation lines to maximise the sellable capacity of the stadium or wrangling data to find the right supporters for your latest marketing campaign, you're expected to do it all.

When the pressure is on and you need to run a promotion to get another few hundred through the turnstiles on a Tuesday night, you deliver. When you go above and beyond to create the final sales push needed to sell out the last few tickets for a crunch fixture that's also on TV, no one at the club understands or appreciates that extra effort. It's just your job, right?

You can see the potential improvements that new technology and software could have on your day-to-day, but then there's the fear of either being the first to use it or having to learn something new. It might not be your own fear holding you back; instead, convincing others at the club to take a leap forward with technology might feel like a never-ending battle.

You're not alone

I know many ticketing folks. They are some of the best generalists I've ever met. They can turn their hand to

INTRODUCTION

anything and create sales out of nothing. The stress of having to make it work time after time after time, however, soon takes its toll. While they see results most of the time, a lot of their work is reactive. There's no time to document processes and no time to plan ahead. A lack of strategy around the ticketing process is costing their club valuable income and costs them their peace.

That is why I've written this book. I want to share my experiences so you know you're not alone, but I also want to equip you with the skills, knowledge and solutions necessary to take control of ticketing and get your ticketing operation firing like it should.

I've been involved in ticketing football matches at all levels: international matches, tournaments, top-of-the-table matches in the Premier League, relegation battles in the fourth tier of non-league and everything in between. All come with their own challenges, but the reality is that the further down the pyramid you go, the harder the job is.

After Wembley Stadium was knocked down to be rebuilt, I spent five years ticketing international England matches on the road and got to see first-hand how different ticketing managers at the top clubs went about their work. I spent four seasons at Tottenham Hotspur at a time when they'd just got back into European competitions and then spent three years at Ticketmaster, where I learned to join the dots between box office operations and the technology that supports them. I launched Kaizen Ticketing in 2014, determined to put all of that learning to good use. So far we've worked with more than 130 football clubs in England – helping many of them to sell digital tickets for the first time in their history.

It's an exciting time for clubs outside of the top flight. Technology is making it easier to do things that were simply not feasible for them a few years ago. Everything from having a huge social media presence to selling a wide variety of products online, such as tickets and sponsorship, just as efficiently as a top-tier club, to digital marketing and building a database of loyal supporters is possible for any club at any level now. There are no excuses for not doing so. The playing field is as level as it's ever been and with the growing trend of fans choosing English Football League (EFL) or non-league matches for their live football fix over Premier League games, there has never been a more important time to get your ticketing strategy in place.

How this book can help

This book is for you if you resonate with any of the challenges I've mentioned. If you're responsible for ticketing a football club outside of the top flight and you sometimes feel overwhelmed, understaffed or generally a bit stuck for new ideas, then I'm confident that this book will be a resource you can keep coming back to for inspiration. I've found it surprising that no one has ever

INTRODUCTION

tried to create something to help their peers navigate the daily challenges they have to deal with in the job. This is my attempt to do just that. In fact, I've seen and experienced so much in my time that it would be selfish of me not to share this knowledge with you.

We're going to put an action plan together as you read through these pages, and you'll be ready to implement it as soon as you finish the final page. You will be well prepared for the additional work that comes with any success and progression on the pitch, and you will have all the tools to create a progressive, high-achieving ticketing function to support your club.

Over the following ten chapters, I'll take you from overwhelm to clarity by teaching you the steps you need to take to achieve operational excellence. I'll cover the tactical elements you'll need to consider and give you a framework to help you with longer-term strategic planning. Whether you're on the frontline or setting the strategy behind the scenes, there is lots in this book to get you thinking.

The book is organised in two parts: in Chapter One to Chapter Six, the tactical part of the book, we'll look at my five C's framework and how it can help you and your club; in Chapter Seven to Chapter Ten we'll look at your strategy to improve ticketing sales in your club. Throughout the book, there are case studies, and I have also provided takeaway tasks that will help you put some of these ideas into practice as you go.

ALL TICKET

There are also some additional resources to supplement the book. These can be downloaded here: www.kaizenticketing.com/resources.

I'm excited for you and the opportunities that you have the potential to uncover.

Let's get started.

ONE
The Brutal Truth

Ticket selling is probably the most generalist job I've known. There's a lot of pressure on you to be an expert in multiple areas, such as customer service, predicting busy periods for staff planning, recruitment to replace the revolving door of match day staff, diplomacy, internal politics, accounting and revenue reporting.

More recently, you're also expected to be an expert in user experience, digital marketing, troubleshooting your supporters' mobile and internet quirks, system integrations, turnstile scanning and using AI and what that means for everyone's future – and you've not had any training. No wonder you're feeling overwhelmed.

You're expected to create, update and circulate detailed reports to the senior management and owners on the hour every hour, but you've been given a laptop from 1996 to do your best work on.

The most difficult part of this scenario to accept is that your job is way harder than it needs to be and through no fault of your own. If clubs are serious about moving with the times and embracing new technologies, it's essential that you're set up for success. The first and most basic step in doing that is making sure you're working with tools that make life easier and don't hinder you.

There's no point in having the latest technology if you haven't had any training on how to use it. You don't need to have a developer-level understanding of modern technology, but I do think it's important that you're given the right level of training to be comfortable using it in your day-to-day. It's an investment in a club's staff and an indirect investment in the fan experience if the people they deal with are comfortable with the tools they have to work with.

The dungeon

It's not uncommon for the ticket office in football stadiums to be affectionately known as 'the dungeon'. This is something I've seen throughout my career and I've had the pleasure of working in quite a few.

Back in the day, my first ever ticketing job was at Wembley Stadium – the old one with the twin towers, before they knocked it all down. The stadium ticketing team were located in an office that was at the base of the right tower as you looked at it down Wembley Way. Sounds iconic, maybe even a tad glamorous, right? Wrong.

Our office backed onto the men's toilets on the concourse, which from time to time would have plumbing issues and tended to leak through the wall and down onto the carpet by the office door. Jumping over the patch as you walked through the door in the morning soon became an unconscious action if you had worked in the office for more than six weeks. In fairness, we didn't have events at the stadium every week, so the patch would come and go month to month.

'Ah well, it's an old stadium and we're knocking it down next year...' was the justification for doing nothing about it. I saw it as a one-off experience and thought I'd never have to work in the dungeon again once we all moved on and they knocked the iconic venue down. Wrong again.

After a detour via the FA, my next stop was Tottenham Hotspur. It was a different dungeon this time and a far cry from the luxury that my former colleagues now find themselves working in in one of the most modern stadiums in the world.

The White Hart Lane dungeon didn't have any patches in the carpet, the plumbing was decent and we weren't located near the men's toilet. It was, however, detached from the rest of the stadium, located in the car park, and had drab mustard-yellow walls that looked like they had last been painted in the late '70s (I started there in 2006). Every other department at the club was located in the purpose-built offices inside the stadium. A trip to the dungeon was something that only happened if one of the staff *really* needed something from us. Otherwise, we were pretty much left alone.

I thought we'd struck it lucky a year later when I heard that they were going to be moving us to the other side of the stadium in our own 'purpose-built' facility. You can imagine my horror when I discovered it was a Portakabin in a car park, with grilles over the windows to protect the equipment inside. When I questioned why the club didn't invest a bit more in the department, which generated millions in revenue every year, I was told that they had – it was a luxury Portakabin. To this day, I still can't tell you what was luxury about it.

There you have it – I've lived it too. If you're reading this from your dungeon, I salute you. Now let's get back on track and talk about where you are and where we're going to get you to.

Poor ticket sales

You might find yourself under some pressure because of poor ticket sales. There can often be a bit of pressure from 'upstairs' when this is happening. The pressure gets passed further down the food chain until the buck stops with you. This is dangerous, as what can often happen here is a reaction in a state of panic.

Someone might say 'Ticket sales aren't great, so we're going to throw a load of things at it and see what sticks.' The problem here is that when you do see something working, you have no idea what it is because you're running a load of the same but different promotions at the same time, with no way of knowing how one thing may or may not have influenced the other. The end result? You guess at what you *think* worked, and then you're surprised when that same thing doesn't work so well next time.

At some point someone may have the idea that you don't need to worry about a strategy of your own: 'Let's just take a look at other clubs like us in our league, the league above and maybe even the league below. It can't be that hard, it's just selling tickets at the end of the day...' This is where it starts to go badly wrong. The most common questions I am asked by all of the clubs we work with are 'What is everyone else doing that we're not but should?' and 'What is [insert specific club who appear to be doing well at the time] doing?'

Now, I don't think this is terrible. As football clubs, you're not competing with each other when it comes to ticket sales. Getting together and sharing good practice, war stories and learnings should be encouraged. Your bigger threats are where parents choose to spend their money on a Saturday afternoon to keep their kids entertained and where the next generation of fans are deciding to entertain themselves online and offline.

The main problem I have with the strategy of looking at a club and copying what they do is that they're probably just guessing too, or if they do have a well-thought-out strategy that they're executing, it might not be relevant for you. By all means, get inspiration from your peers, but just because something has worked for them, there's no guarantee that it'll be effective for you.

Not selling tickets online

Why am I so intent on making sure you have your strategy in place? Surely, as a supplier of ticketing systems, all I should care about is selling you some shiny new tech and bragging about how many clubs are now using it. While that might be OK for some, I want better for you – and, selfishly, if we get you thinking strategically about how you sell tickets, you will sell more. That way, we all win.

Importantly, you need to be ready for when the club is successful on the pitch too. Another common myth is that it'll all get better and work itself out 'when we go up'. Wrong.

Your attendances and revenue will increase – that is certain – but so will the workload and the expectations, both internally and from the fans. If you haven't got solid foundations in place at that point, you're probably going to be in for more stress, more frustration and have a higher staff turnover to deal with in the process.

This is where the club infrastructure has to be right and set up to support you in your role. 'Infrastructure' – it sounds way more complicated than it is. What I'm really saying here is you need to have whatever you need to be able to do the basics well. You need to be set up like a modern organisation.

Let's start with the absolute basics – selling tickets online.

I can't believe I had to write that, but yes, until fairly recently, not all football clubs in the EFL were selling tickets online. We're making progress in the EFL – at the time of writing, all seventy-two football clubs sell tickets online. If you go one league below, in the National League, all bar one are doing it. As you go further down, the number of clubs that aren't selling online increases drastically; unfortunately, there is still a significant shift in mindset needed.

'Why do we need to bother to sell online if we don't sell out?', 'We have a lot of older fans', 'We lose money if we sell online. We might as well just take cash only', 'Our fans don't trust the internet.' These are all common excuses not to change that I have heard when I've spoken to football clubs over the last few years. Ridiculous,

I know, but that is how some people are still thinking about online sales – at all levels.

It's usually the clubs where this mindset is prevalent that struggle with lots of on-day sales. There's a token option to buy in advance online, but it's not efficient. Fans struggle to buy or, even worse, lose confidence in the process, so they decide to just turn up on the day and pay in person. I've seen this a fair bit in the EFL. It's not just about ticking the box to say you're selling online. If it's not being done well, it's almost as bad as not doing it at all.

You're also missing out on the impulse purchasers. You know the people who always say 'Oh I must go and watch my local team this season' and never do? They never do, because either it's too hard to buy a ticket or you're out of sight and out of mind. Except for once a year when you do a big promotion because numbers are falling and everyone at the club is having a mild panic about increasing sales.

Can you see the pattern yet?

The consequences

With all of this in mind, let me explain the three key consequences of everything I've laid out in this chapter.

Your club is losing money

The less attention you give to how well (or not) you're selling tickets online, the more money you are losing. Not only are you losing money, but also you're missing out on collecting money earlier. All of those supporters who turn up at 2.50pm on a Saturday afternoon to buy a ticket could be giving you their hard-earned cash days or even weeks earlier if you made it easier for them to. You could use that cash sooner. Imagine how happy your CFO would be with that improved cash flow.

This isn't a dig at people working at the club already. Everyone is doing their best. To ask a commercial manager or ticketing manager with no experience of designing software, however, to improve the user experience of a digital product makes as much sense as hiring an accountancy firm to build you a house.

I'm sure some would tell you they can do the job, but it's not their speciality. This is where the problem starts. They say 'How hard can it be?', 'Well I think this, so must everyone else...' and that's where the process starts to deteriorate.

You need a specialist with an objective viewpoint, and experience and thorough research behind them – not the opinion of someone who is too close to the problem. That might be hard to hear, but it's the truth. A commercial manager specialises in bringing in lucrative commercial deals to benefit the club and a ticket office manager should specialise in running a ticketing operation. Both are important people to consult when building a ticketing system or adding features, but building software on opinion is a guaranteed way to fail. A football club can become a bit of a bubble, so having people who can look beyond the day-to-day and week-to-week activities will help you to plan for the future and ask challenging questions.

The clubs that are getting this right are setting themselves up like software companies. I've seen this evolve over the last four to five years. They are creating positions never previously seen at football clubs – like user experience designers or supporter engagement managers, digital marketers, data analysts and product managers. At the top-tier clubs, we're even seeing software architects and chief technology officers. These are the specialists who will work with people like you, whose great understanding of the club and its supporters will get you the best results digitally. Don't overlook the importance of this concept, which I'll expand on throughout the book. I know resources aren't unlimited below the Premier League, but you do still have options to use these specialist skills through people or tools. I'll go into this more in later chapters.

The fans aren't happy

How many of you read that and then muttered 'They never are...'? That's what we're going to fix. It's not new news that fan expectations are getting higher and higher every season, particularly when it comes to how fans interact with the club online.

We are all looking for better digital experiences. Some industries have nailed it and naturally a fan will expect this of their football club too. Some people expect an app, others want to be able to check out in one click, and there will be some fans who expect you to know who they are and what they like and where they like to sit based on previous activity.

This also goes for when and how you communicate with them. The options are plentiful: SMS, emails, push notifications, social media or old-school methods like post or phone calls. Everyone has their preferences, and you are in the unenviable position of needing to understand each of those preferences at an individual level. We all want this as consumers and it's not unfair for someone to expect their club to adopt the same approach. The days of one-size-fits-all are over, I'm afraid. It's time to do better.

Football clubs are in the unique position of being able to resist making changes in this area over other industries and organisations. If I have a bad experience shopping at Tesco, I'll go to Sainsbury's. If I get fed up with that or don't like something, I'll give Morrisons a try. Football is different. Fans are programmed to stick with their club through thick and thin. You put the price of their season ticket up every year and the fans moan, threaten to not come back – but they do. Year after year after year. The team go on a losing streak and haven't won a match for five games back-to-back. The fans still turn up for the sixth. Going down the road to your rival club because they're playing better, are a bit cheaper etc hasn't ever been an option.

I say that, but I have seen that attitude change at the top end of the game over the last few years. Ever since we've been making it easier for lower-league clubs to attract fans, sell advance tickets and get themselves out there on social media, I have seen fans adopting another club – mainly because they are fed up with the lack of appreciation for the fans at some of the clubs at the top level.

There's the warning. People won't put up with it forever and the more you can do to keep up with the ever-evolving expectations, the more loyal your supporter base becomes. You'll need and appreciate them through the hard times.

You're struggling to find and keep good-quality people

This is like the internal version of the previous point. If you're not investing in decent working tools for the staff, they'll start to look elsewhere. Granted, it's a dream to work at a football club for a lot of people, but some clubs may have taken advantage of that and been a little slow to go over and above for the staff.

A few reliable, capable members of ticket office staff – whether they're full-time or work only on match days – can make the difference as to how ticketing at the club is perceived by the fans. If you find good ticketing people, take care of them, as they are a rare breed.

As much fun as it can be to work in football, being moaned at, verbally abused and having to repeatedly apologise for something out of your control takes its toll on you. Going into work on a match day, dreading what lies in wait for you is no fun and it's no surprise that at many clubs staff turnover in the ticket office can be high. It's not just a money thing – we all know that ticket office work isn't always the best paid, for match day staff in particular. Why is it, though, that some clubs manage to retain the same people season after season and other clubs feel like they're having to bring in new staff every other month?

Creating a calm, controlled environment is key – one where staff are confident in the software that they use and where they're not having to apologise to every supporter because the system crashed, they can't find their order, they've accidentally sold their seat to someone else or their computer is being painfully slow as they try to sell the supporter a ticket for the match. Software choices play a part, but so does infrastructure: modern computers, good Wi-Fi and training that lets staff feel like they can confidently field questions about upcoming matches, sales processes and general stadium information.

If you've got great match day staff, match days become easier and, dare I say, fun. It all starts with making their experience a good one and one they're happy to repeat every other Tuesday night and Saturday. Simple things go a long way and we'll look at some ways we can help you to build a confident ticketing team as we get into further chapters.

A much-needed change

Real ticketing people have the strongest can-do attitudes of any profession I've known. We just make do with what we've got and continually create miracles out of nothing. How many of you, though, can hand on heart say you've had decent training that has helped you to achieve any of the following?

- Improve fan experience
- Deliver top-tier customer service
- Become confident with technology or, at the least, basic computer skills
- Understand the basics of buyer psychology – online and in person
- Create digital marketing campaigns that work or ads that convert

As you read through these pages, my aim is to help address some of this with you. We will start by making sure the right foundations are in place by giving you the tools and the confidence to get the right people at your club together and discussing the right things – keeping them focussed on what matters.

We will be getting tactical. I will share some of the things I've seen work and tactics I've used myself to create captivating offers and compelling reasons for supporters to buy and come back again.

I'll help you to get comfortable with some of the technology choices that are available to you today. Don't worry if things feel overwhelming in that area – by the end of that chapter, you'll be asking all of the right questions of your suppliers that will help to cut through all of the noise.

As we go further into the book, we will get you set up to start planning strategically too. We will look at the important areas that require long-term thinking: everything from communicating with and involving your supporters around the big decisions through to creating a strategy document for your club, something that everyone can get behind, review and improve as you turn the ticketing function at your club into a revenue-generating powerhouse.

As we have seen, for many ticketing folks the job can feel like it's harder than it needs to be. You're fighting to do your best for the club and the supporters, but obstacle after obstacle is being put in your way. Being the diligent and resolute professional that you are, however, you find a way to blast through these roadblocks and deliver week in, week out.

The frustration is real, but we keep coming back – week after week, season after season. I've worked with many ticketing people over the years and the one common thread that comes up when we've had a good chat about some of the challenges they're facing is this: the job seems harder than it needs to be because there is no real ticketing strategy or direction. It's left up to them to try and figure something out, which, more often than not, leaves them reacting to the latest problems rather than implementing new ideas and initiatives.

TWO
Clarity

Now we've set the scene and talked about the possible constraints that might be holding you back, let's start thinking about solutions.

I appreciate that fixing some of these problems sounds easier said than done. You're under immense pressure to do five things at once, all day every day – and I hear that. I'm also going to argue, however, that if you pause and take some time now to think about this stuff, some of those tasks will no longer seem as important. Better still, they might even magically disappear from your workload.

The importance of planning

A little bit of planning and preparation will go a long way towards solving your problems. In this chapter, we're going to look at what tasks you're doing and find out whether you need to be doing them or there's a better way to approach the ticketing process. Taking time now will be worth it in the long run. It's time to take control back and get your ticketing operation firing like it should be.

Unfortunately, this is where I see things going wrong over the years. People whip themselves into a frenzy and are then too busy to plan or create a ticketing strategy, but if they took the time to plan one out, they'd instantly create time for themselves just by gaining a degree of control.

Once you have a plan, you'll stop chasing your tail. You'll be able to come to a decision about what is important for now and what can get put to one side for the time being. You'll have alignment across the club and the noise that you're getting from other areas will be good noise because you're all invested in achieving the same thing.

We're going to free you from that awful feeling of being faced with never-ending to-do lists, of starting the day on the backfoot, and that horrible feeling of being undervalued by everyone else at the club. We're going to turn you instead into the woman or man with the plan and get you leading from the front.

So, on the subject of having the plan. When it comes to your current situation, you might be at the mercy of your marketing team or person who looks after marketing at the club. Depending on their experience, they could be a strong ally or a source of frustration. What isn't helpful is just trying stuff aimlessly to see what sticks. This is sometimes justified as 'experimentation', but it really doesn't help anyone.

Controlling experimentation

Just to be clear: experiments are great as long as you know what you're doing, by which I mean having an initial, well-thought-out hypothesis that you're testing, setting some criteria for the test and setting a metric or two that will determine success or failure ahead of getting started. If you're not doing that, then, unfortunately, you're wasting your time.

We're going to learn how to do these experiments in a controlled way. Maybe you can teach the marketing department a thing or two the next time they ask you for twenty-five versions of the same promo code that need to be shared in the next ten minutes. Now, depending on the level your club is at, the marketing department could consist of a team, an individual (who is probably also doing social media posts, designing graphics, managing the website and a bit of partner activation thrown in for good measure) or a volunteer who is helping out alongside their full-time job.

Regardless, we have to remember that everyone is trying to do their best. If we can get you to a point where you're working well together, you'll be a formidable partnership. You'll be working to improve the same metrics and have the same answer to the key question 'Is this important for now?' That will naturally help you to focus only on the needle-moving campaigns.

Your conversations will move away from them telling you that you need to do X, Y and Z with no context through to a more collaborative, two-way conversation where you discuss how close you are to achieving the target that you've set together.

Achieving targets

How do we get to that point? Well, over the years I've spent working with clubs, I've seen these challenges show themselves in various guises. As Kaizen became more of a trusted partner, clubs slowly started to ask for help, advice or just a few tips on how to get more people buying tickets or existing fans spending a bit more.

I slowly started to see that when we helped clubs to get a focus on what they wanted to achieve in the short term (ie within six to eighteen months) it was easier for them to plan their activity and things became less chaotic for them. That evolved into helping them to create longer-term strategies and short-term tactics for compelling offers through the season while making the best use of the software that we were providing. Some of the longer-term initiatives turned into roadmap items for our software, so we grew as they did. As that started to play out and have a positive impact on their sales, the next natural area they asked about was communicating consistently with fans and ticketing best practices in general.

Introducing the five C's

Those years of experience led to the creation of the five C's methodology. Five steps we go through with a club that asks for help. I've never formalised it in writing, publicly, like I am doing in this book – it's been an organic process where one stage led to the next. While it might look like a nice linear set of steps on paper, however, the reality is you'll find yourself hopping back to an area to update it as you learn more information in another.

The five C's are:

1. Clarity
2. Captivate

3. Cutting-edge tech
4. Communication
5. Confidence

It all starts with clarity. A problem well defined is a problem half solved.

If you're not clear on your aims and the problem you want to fix, no one else will be either. Even worse, you might have different people around the club with different goals, all working individually to achieve them. If they're conflicting or don't complement each other, everyone fails.

As you are the person in charge of ticketing, I'm going to challenge you to own this one if you don't already. This is the first, and arguably the most important, step in minimising the chaos and noise from your day-to-day, but you're going to have to take ownership of the situation.

The good news is that this isn't something you need to do in isolation – it's a team game. You are, however, going to be the person who drives the change and keeps everyone else aligned. First and foremost, as a club, you need to be able to answer the following question: 'From a ticketing perspective, where do we want to be in the next [up to eighteen] months?'

If I'm planning this out with a club, I'll always try and steer clear of getting into too much detail beyond eighteen months. Football is a unique business, as you'll already know. It only takes a player sale, the loss of a manager, a bad run of form or, conversely, the emergence of a superstar, the team clicking and a few favourable decisions to find yourself in the league below or above.

That can drastically change what is possible and what will be required in terms of your ticketing function. Budgets can suddenly appear or be slashed overnight, as can the number of people in your team. Planning for where you currently are, with an eye on what might happen in the short term if you go up or down, is the sensible approach.

Not wanting to jump too far ahead here, but technology shouldn't be part of the conversation just yet. This is probably the easiest way to go off-piste at this stage of our process: 'We've seen this club have that feature and this other club with another feature, we should be doing that too.' If the conversation starts to go this way, pull it back to focussing on outcomes. If you can articulate the outcome you want to achieve, the choice of technology needed to do that will work itself out later in the process. This is much easier said than done when you open the conversation up to others around the club.

It's natural to want to dive into systems, features, new, exciting and emerging technologies and think about the possibilities. The reality that no one tells you is that doing that at this stage only complicates things – you end up with solutions looking for problems and, even worse, inventing problems to justify your new technology choices.

Approaching tech in the right way

As the owner of a technology company, it might come as a surprise that I'm saying this, but it's the truth. During our sales process, I want to have a chat about what a club is hoping our product can do in relation to a future aspiration they have. If the person I'm talking to dives straight into the tech and can't tell me what they're hoping to achieve or what problems they need to fix, I'll politely ask if we can address that first. There have been a couple of occasions where that request has been completely ignored – and in that case, I'll suggest that we're probably not the right match and move on. The hard truth is that it'll be painful for both sides over the long term if you don't have clarity over your goals. It's the equivalent of getting into your car and driving aimlessly for an hour and then complaining that you're not at the destination where you thought you would be at.

Historically, football clubs have been a little slower to adopt over the years. Everyone is waiting for someone to go first. Eventually, someone does and then everyone else follows relatively quickly. I've seen it over the years with ticket scanning at automated turnstiles; the transition from season ticket voucher books to plastic cards and, more recently, from cards to mobile tickets; and transitioning to digital programmes or having a cashless stadium.

There is nothing wrong with taking inspiration from other clubs – taking ideas and making them work for your situation can be healthy. Too many times, though, new initiatives are introduced because the club down the road did it and it seemed to work for them. As I said in the previous chapter, you need to ask yourself if it is the right thing for you and, more importantly, if it is it the right thing for now. If it is, how are you measuring the impact that it's having – how will you know if it has been a success for you?

Tracking progress

It's a good idea to articulate what you want to achieve in a way that allows you to track your progress. A simple way to do that is to include a time frame or a trackable number. That way, you'll be able to get the right level of focus from everyone who is contributing to improving the areas that you've identified.

Capturing your goal in a simple statement is a good starting point. You might replace 'We want to sell more season tickets' with 'We want to increase our season ticket sales by 500 by the start of the season.' Rather than saying 'We want more people coming to games', you could get more specific by saying 'We want our average league game attendances to be 5,500 by the end of the season.'

I've mentioned a few times that you'll need to discuss these priorities, but who should you be discussing them with? This is a great opportunity for you to take the initiative and lead on it if no one is doing this already.

It starts off with a bit of empathy. You need to think about what ticketing should contribute to the club from a few different perspectives. What does the CEO or general manager need from your area this season? The safety officer might be getting some pressure from the advisory group on ticketing-related issues. Perhaps ticketing revenue is a key driver for future plans and the CFO is looking to create as many wins as possible to help drive that forward.

This is your opportunity to look at your area from a strategic viewpoint and think about how what you focus on can inform the overall perspective.

Looking at the bigger picture

It's easy for departments to see challenges from just one point of view. Getting together and sharing those different points of view is a common thing at most clubs – update meetings and pre-match planning happens frequently – but the thing I've always taken away from those types of meetings is that the attitude can be about making sure 'my area is OK'. The slight tweak I'm suggesting here is a bit more of a shared ownership of these initiatives, where everyone involved has a responsibility to contribute to their success.

You will likely find that there is a bit of crossover when it comes to these priorities. It won't take long for everyone to realise that while the motivations across the different areas of the club might be different, the outcomes that everyone wants will be similar at worst or identical at best. It's usually once that has been recognised that everyone can see that football's a team sport off the pitch too.

I must stress the importance of involving people from the different areas of the club during this process. It might be tempting to go through it in isolation or with just one or two people from similar or related areas at the club. In many ways, it would be easier to keep it that way – you'll all probably agree with each other and feel like you're getting somewhere a lot more quickly.

The difficulty will come a bit later as you start to try and implement some of your new ideas and changes. There will have been no buy-in and no warning, and we all know how most people tend to react when things are sprung on them.

ALL TICKET

It will feel harder early on and definitely a little slower before it feels like things are moving, but you'll have far more success in implementing worthwhile change if you have a balanced view from across the club when it comes to your ticketing strategy. Everyone has an opinion when it comes to ticketing, both internally and externally. When something goes wrong, everyone is a ticketing expert.

Fans are quick to tell the club what they should have done instead, and your peers are no different. Now is the time to let them have their say and work with them to help them understand your world a bit better. I know that sounds like more hassle than it will be worth, but trust me. I've lost count of the number of times that I've seen this play out and people openly admit that they didn't fully appreciate how tough it is or how many interrelated things ticketing folks have to manage, balance or generally be involved in. You'll gain new-found respect from your peers by exposing them to some of that, I promise. Give it a try.

External opinion can also be helpful as you start to make your internal plans. Many clubs will start with a survey if they want to know what is most important to supporters. They will then use this information to guide the internal discussion as they get clear on the areas they want to focus on and improve.

CASE STUDY: Southend United – A new beginning started with a survey

A great case study that shows the benefit of gathering thoughts and opinions before setting a new direction is Southend United, a client of ours at Kaizen. After many troubled years off the pitch, the club came into new ownership in 2024.

During the takeover negotiations, the club's commercial manager, Rylee Doe, commissioned a survey so the new owners could hear what was most important to supporters. This allowed them to prioritise the list of things to improve around the club.

Here's the process they went through in Rylee's own words:

'One of the first things that the owners acknowledged was that we didn't know anything about how the fans felt about different aspects of the club. We decided to run a survey so we could use data to our advantage.

'It took almost three months of preparation as we wanted to make sure all aspects of the club were covered, from the club shop to the toilets. While it was a lot of work, it was completely worth it as we knew it would give us a blueprint in terms of where to start along with some potential quick wins.'

The survey was welcomed by the supporters with over 1,700 responses, which Rylee could take to the new owners and use to highlight some of the obvious areas that needed attention. He said, 'The number of responses was phenomenal. We had benchmarked 300 as our "high-confidence" number, so to get that many really helped us to see the obvious patterns. Some areas needed financial investment in the stadium, such as the toilets. Others were easier wins, like having food trucks outside the stadium in response to some supporters wanting catering options outside the ground.'

The survey had a massive commercial impact too. Rylee went on to say, 'We were able to approach new potential partners, knowing some of the things that supporters were looking for. We were going into conversations with reliable data. We also saw huge improvements in our hospitality offerings and sales. After renovating one of the lounges, we saw an 80% increase in sales in that area.

'We're now selling out our hospitality areas in advance since that investment too. We went from just three matches sold out in advance to nineteen. The demand was there and listening to the feedback from our supporters has helped us to deliver the product that they really wanted.'

We'll get into more details on surveys in later chapters. To get things moving internally, you may need to start with a series of the same conversations with different people separately at first. Then, as you start to gather opinion and potentially conflicting ideas, arrange to get those parties together so the discussion can be had and priorities agreed.

If you're starting from scratch, these are the people and/or areas I'd kick the conversations off with:

- CEO
- General manager/operations
- Finance department
- Safety officer
- Marketing and media department
- Commercial/hospitality department

And the wildcard:

- Club secretary

The club secretary is often overlooked when it comes to ticketing. Most of the time, they don't get involved in ticketing issues, unless it's agreeing pricing with your opposition for cup matches or fixture changes. They can, however, be a great resource for finding out what the general feeling is around the club. They're involved in so many areas, they'll know what the board are focussing on strategically, they'll know the bugbears of the CEO and, in many cases, they'll know the club inside out just due to the sheer breadth of their role. Don't overlook this often untapped resource. I've given you the outline of your first ticketing strategy workshop agenda in the additional resources, so check those out too.

A final word on focus

When it comes to everyone's strategy, there are two things it will come down to:

1. Getting more fans into the stadium
2. Generating more revenue from the fans that are already coming

Now, the secret to getting this right is picking which one you want to focus on. Whenever I start working with a club, we'll talk around ticketing strategies in different forms and it'll generally result in me asking which one of these two things they want to focus on.

I think I might have a 100% record on the answer – if it's not 100%, it's definitely not lower than 95%. More often than not, the answer that comes back is 'Both.' Which, unfortunately, is not the answer that is going to help us make progress.

Remember, we're talking about focus. The strategies you use to achieve one don't always complement the other. You need to pick one (for now), get skilled at improving that and, when you've got yourself to a point that you're happy with, you can then switch your attention to the other.

There's nothing to stop you switching back and forth and you can do that a few times through the season – see these as 'mini campaigns' over a few months at a time.

CLARITY

Just because you're intensely pursuing improvements in one area doesn't mean the other will be forgotten forever – you're just prioritising. By doing that, you're making sure you get the best result possible.

I can't emphasise enough how important it is to make sure you arrange to meet regularly to review the priorities that you've now identified. There will come a time when you agree that you've done enough or a change of focus is needed. Not taking the time to review will likely result in you plugging away at the same thing longer than necessary, which, in turn, will result in people losing interest and then going off and doing their own thing anyway – so keep these initiatives fairly short and sharp. By that I'd be thinking of two to four months per campaign depending on what it is and whether you're building on something that is existing or starting from scratch.

Here's your first takeaway task.

> **TAKEAWAY TASK: Staff brainstorm**
>
> Make a list of the people in key roles around the club. Make it your business to have a conversation with each of them and find out what they want or expect from ticketing as a function at the club. Push them to be specific. Get them to think both tactically in the short term and more strategically over the long term.

THREE
Captivate

Congratulations – just completing the first step in gaining some clarity means that you're already more structured than most. Let's keep the momentum going.

Don't forget to do the hard bit and make sure you've involved the *right* people – not just the people you *want* to involve. It's the hardest part because of the number of initial ideas, opinions and contrasting beliefs, but once you work through those, you should start to feel a sense of cohesiveness and it will be far easier to say no to the things that aren't right for now.

Now you're clear on the important stuff, you get to have a bit of fun. This is where you can start to plan out some ideas for what you're going to do to try and improve the things that you've identified as a group. Like in the previous step, you're going to make sure that you hold yourself accountable for the outcome that you're seeking, what you expect to happen and what good looks like in your context. I'll share a framework for doing this with you shortly.

Before we get to that, I'd recommend that you have the things that you've decided you want to focus on documented and visible to everyone in the club. The simple act of having them where you're likely to see them every day is a nice, subtle reminder of what is going to move the needle and another way of helping everyone to maintain focus on the important things and keep the right perspective when it's tempting to drop everything for the next big trend or perceived emergency.

Solve problems but avoid overwhelm

Deciding on what you're going to do to solve problems, like our previous step, requires collaboration. As the ticketing expert, you should definitely drive this. You're also going to need buy-in and support from some of your allies around the club and, depending on what you're planning, you might need a bit of external support from your suppliers and partners too. This is also where you may naturally come together with the marketing team to create that formidable partnership I mentioned earlier. If marketing doesn't exist as a function in its own right at your club, this could be input from colleagues working in the media department or the commercial side of things, or you may just have to be formidable on your own and let everyone else marvel at your initiative and endeavour.

The main thing you need to keep in mind is that whatever you choose to do, it needs to tie back to what you're ultimately trying to achieve for the club.

Let's say season tickets are your focus and, using the statement from the previous chapter, your internal focus is 'We want to increase our season ticket sales by 500 by the start of the season.' It would make little sense (at this point) to introduce things such as the ability to pre-order a half-time pie and pint, a new club mobile app, a 'build your own' style mini package of six games or a new merchandise range including mugs, stationery and pin badges.

I'm hoping you're reading this and thinking, *Of course not, Dave, none of these things are going to get more people buying season tickets*. Yes, you would be correct.

This is, unfortunately, how it plays out in the real world: 'This app company got in touch and said they'd give us a good price if we agree to work with them by the end of the month', 'The team down the road are doing half-time pre-orders, so we should as well', 'Our software provider has just released this new package feature, so we should use it. Better use everything, just in case we're missing something', 'Our new merchandise partner can do a new range, so what do we have to lose?'

This is how it starts to go wrong. All of these statements are valid, but none of these outcomes are going to massively contribute to selling more season tickets. This is why keeping focus is more important than ever. As Steve Jobs said on stage at WWDC '97, 'Focussing is about saying no.' It doesn't have to be a hard no – there's nothing wrong with a 'not right now'.[1]

Instead, what initiatives could you run, keeping your goal of 500 more season tickets in mind? Here are some ideas:

- Outreach to local retailers or club partners to negotiate special benefits for season ticket holders
- Invite season ticket holders to bring a friend for free a few times a season
- Review or extend early-bird pricing periods to make them more favourable
- Explore payment options to give people more ways to pay or pay in instalments
- Curate a series of non-football events that will be offered to season ticket holders only

1. Z Mejia, 'Steve Jobs: Here's what most people get wrong about focus', CNBC (2 October 2018), www.cnbc.com/2018/10/02/steve-jobs-heres-what-most-people-get-wrong-about-focus.html, accessed 29 May 2025

- Research whether families buy season tickets and see if there's anything stopping them

This should all feel painfully obvious and rightly so. The key to getting this right is doing the basics well and that's exactly what I'm advocating here – staying focussed on the things that will move you forward or contribute towards the impact that you want to make.

Even when we're helping clubs to get into more advanced tactics, I'm quick to remind everyone that we should never stop doing the basics. You can only build on good foundations.

The other thing I want to call out here is making sure you don't feel the pressure to try and tackle everything at once. In keeping with what I've been saying about focus, the other challenge you may face is overwhelm.

If you've never done an exercise like the one in the previous chapter, it's likely that quite a few areas that you want to address as a club have surfaced. You would be wise to prioritise these with your team then pick one or two to address and improve. Trying to address everything at once will likely lead to the feeling of even more chaos internally and give mixed messages to the fans.

People accept and process change at different rates, so my advice would be to meet people where they are. Get them comfortable with your new initiatives gradually and as they start to see the benefits for themselves, you can start to do more.

Tie the action to the problem

Now you've decided what you're going to start with, and you've got some ideas on what you can do to make a positive change or improvement in that area, you should think about how you're going to present that so you can measure progress along the way.

Consider how you're going to be accountable for the success or failure of implementing that new thing. Often, the missing component is a metric. If I ask someone what they're measuring or how they'll know if the implementation of a new idea has gone well, I'll often get something like 'We're still figuring that bit out' as the response.

Here is a simple framework to help that become a thing of the past. The new way will create shared accountability and genuine discussion about what good looks like for you. That way, everyone has bought into the same outcome from the start and if things aren't going to plan, you can have a conversation about that and think about possible ideas to get back on track.

All you need to do is to take the draft statement I have supplied below and tailor it to your club's needs and goals. Your statement should be simple and written in a language that anyone working at the club can understand and contribute to.

- **Draft statement**: We believe that by [doing the thing], we will [specific outcome]. We'll know that this has been a success because we will see [an increase/decrease in your agreed metric] by [agreed time period].

- **Tailored statement**: We believe that by [introducing direct debit as a payment option], we will [sell more season tickets this summer]. We'll know that this has been a success because we will see [our season ticket sales increase by 10%] by [the opening day of the new season].

This will get you out of the mindset of (in this example) introducing direct debit payments just because you've seen a few others do it and want to know if it's any good. That may still be the initial reason for considering it, but now you're going to have agreement on what good looks like for your club or what specific purpose it should have for you.

Maybe you're already at your maximum with season ticket sales and you see direct debit as a key way of retaining the existing supporters. Great – let's define that as success and discuss the metric that makes implementing it worthwhile. You'll now be starting to see how you can use this.

Using this framework brings more clarity to your internal conversations. You all know and agree on what you're expecting from this and if things aren't performing as you hoped, you can have productive discussions about why you think that's the case and come up with some ideas for things that might help you to get back on track – all done in a way in which everyone is taking some ownership of both good and bad situations.

Software is not always the answer

When it comes to deciding what you're going to do, based on the outcome of your initial internal consultation, you'll realise that you have many choices. Controversially, one of the ideas that I want to share with you is that software isn't always the right option. You can solve or improve many situations without needing to introduce new software or integrations.

That might not be what you were expecting from me. Especially as our next C is all about cutting-edge tech, you might be surprised that I'm advocating for non-technical solutions too.

I'll always look for the quickest and cheapest way to prove a theory before investing more time and often money in developing a solution further. Having this mindset means I don't spend too much time on things that aren't working, I can easily adjust my plan and try again without being wedded to a solution, and, most importantly, I don't waste money on things that people don't want or which don't get the outcome I'm looking for. What this can often mean is that we'll test something in a more manual way first before committing to automating it with technology. This basic approach helps everyone to learn more about the problem and uncover what we didn't know before we got started. This makes building the long-term solution with technology much more efficient, as we're doing it with much improved knowledge of the problem.

This is the secret bit that no one is talking about on LinkedIn, because it's not glamorous, often fails and doesn't give you the opportunity to use the hashtag #innovation after posting about it. The irony is, however, that this is exactly how you innovate. No one guesses right the first time.

What do I mean by this? Let me give you some examples of how you can adopt this mentality and avoid the trap of leading with tech for tech's sake.

Let's imagine that you've agreed that you want to tackle the problem of ticket usage. Season ticket holder attendance rates aren't looking great and, after a bit of research, you find out that people are being choosy about which matches to show up for because the season ticket is such good value. Even if they miss ten matches in a season, it's still cheaper than paying match by match. There's a separate lesson to be learned about pricing for next season, but, in the meantime, your focus is to increase season ticket usage because you're selling out all of your regular match tickets. One of the ways you've identified to increase usage could be allowing season ticket holders to put their ticket up for resale if they're not planning to use it – a great way of making that ticket available to someone else for a single match.

Rather than calling your software supplier and demanding that they build a resale platform in the next four weeks, it might be better to test out the theory first. This way you can see if resale is indeed the right option. It gives you a chance to test aspects of your approach, such as your messaging, the incentive for people to put their tickets up for sale and the mechanics of making the original ticket unavailable.

When we come up with new ideas and initiatives, we don't know what we don't know, and trying it out in a low-cost, manual way first helps us to uncover some of these things before we get into the weeds of building the technical solution.

As a lightweight test in this scenario, you could identify one stand in the ground to test with. You could ask season ticket holders to contact you via email if they want to put their ticket up for sale and keep a manual list of tickets available. You could then sell those tickets as and when they become available and see what the take-up is like.

If you're inundated with demand, then great. This is all the data you need to prove that a more efficient, technical solution is required. If it's a little slower, that's great too. You can now play with the various aspects of the offer. Does it make sense to the fans? Are you incentivising them enough to be bothered to tell you that the ticket can be resold? You can tweak every aspect until you unlock the thing that makes it stick and then worthy of development of a more automated solution.

What is your minimum viable product?

In the software world, this kind of approach is often referred to as the minimum viable product. Starting with this mindset for anything new is a clever approach. You save time, you save money, and you avoid a lot of wasted development effort when it comes to your technology. It's not scalable and deliberately so. Your goal is to test a concept with a small group first to figure out what you don't know or could improve, before going bigger.

Sometimes, the answer isn't a new feature at all. It can be a campaign that the supporters all get behind. Technology can still play a role in supporting the campaign, but what I'm trying to guide you towards is not to lead with tech but to stay focussed on the outcome that you want.

A great example of a campaign that leads with everyone getting behind a number and is then supported by technology is Carlisle United's annual attendance target match. Every season, the club identifies a fixture where they set an attendance target that is a little higher than their average.

They'll publicly state the target on social media, give the match plenty of promotion and get local businesses involved to help them reach the number. In the past few seasons, they've had campaigns such as #8kforMK, centred around a home fixture against Milton Keynes Dons, and #10for10, where tickets were reduced to £10 with the goal of surpassing 10,000 fans in attendance.

Local businesses were able to buy tickets and donate them to local schools as another way of helping to get more people to attend the match. As you can see, this isn't a 'technology first' initiative, just some sensible marketing, excellent social media coverage to get the fans behind it and a robust ticketing system that can handle the demand.

Understand the problem from all angles

Now it's your turn to think about what campaigns you can run to address the problem(s) you've identified. How can you do it in such a way that gets the fans excited about it as well?

A great place to start would be to do a mini audit of what you need to set yourself up for success. By this I mean make sure that you've got good foundations to build on. I touched on it in the first chapter, but this is where not having sound infrastructure in place will limit what you can do.

For example, you can have the most elegant campaign in the world, great social media posts and the most engaging message that the whole community resonates with, but if your website is inconsistent, confusing and clunky, you're not going to benefit from any of the hard work that it's taken to drive people to it.

Here are some starting points for your audit (I've expanded on these in the accompanying resources).

How easy is it for people to buy tickets from you?

If it's a slog for people to buy tickets, your efforts will all be in vain. The obvious place to start is your club website. Is it glaringly obvious where to go to buy a ticket? I feel a bit ridiculous writing that, but I've lost count of the number of times I've been on club websites – usually clubs I think we can help, so I have a nose around before making contact – and it seems like telling people how to buy a ticket is a secret.

After you get your club website doing the basics, how about the site that sells your tickets? Is it clear and easy to use? Do people have the information they need? Think about new fans too. If it's my first time visiting your club, what do I need to know and is that easy for me to find out as I'm looking for tickets to buy?

Have you introduced good practice?

I mentioned earlier that the football clubs thinking like software companies and employing roles that you'd find in them are going to win over the long term – and here is a good example. A user experience designer is an essential role when you're building software – someone with a strong understanding of web design principles and, in more complex scenarios, knowledge of human–computer interaction and consumer psychology.

As a football club, particularly outside of the top tier, you might not have the luxury of being able to afford to hire that person full-time. This is where you can and should lean on your software suppliers. They should be employing people with this skill set. Ask them about their usability testing process, and ask for evidence and details of the research they've done around features in their product. If they either can't or refuse, this is a red flag.

It's so important to get this right. I had some experience of this working as a product manager before launching Kaizen. I then spent a lot of time and a fair amount of cash studying this in depth throughout the first eighteen months of building our product. Software, of course, is never finished, so any new features that are added to a product should go through initial research and planning and then user testing once it's built. Testing with as few as three people will identify up to 80% of the issues, so there's no excuse for skipping this important step.

Please don't fall into the trap of thinking you could do this bit yourself. You're a subject matter expert, but you're not a software professional. Having someone who can look at something objectively, carry out research with fans or test without any bias can be the difference between creating an average and a great user experience. I can't emphasise the importance of this enough.

Have you considered accessibility?

While we're on the subject of good practice, I also want to put web accessibility on your radar. This is often overlooked, but remember that some of your supporters will have accessibility needs when they use your services online. Some may be using screen readers, while others may have other visual impairments. I've shared some additional resources in the workbook, but just basic things like making sure you're not using colour as the only way to identify things online – eg prices on a seating plan – will go a long way.

Are solutions internally aligned?

Some people may tell you that there's no point in trying to come up with captivating offers, great value packages or clever promotions, because people will only buy tickets if the team is playing well. Don't listen to this. If it were true, every relegated team would be playing in an empty stadium every season, and that just doesn't happen. You'll naturally have more demand for tickets if the team is playing attractive football and winning regularly, but don't fall into the trap of not trying to push sales if the team is struggling for form.

I've worked with teams that have recorded some of their highest attendances on record during a performance slump or increased season ticket sales the season after a disappointing relegation. Don't doubt the power of an offer that gets the fans interested, feels like good value for money and is so good, it's almost impossible to not want to take it up. Your job is to uncover what that looks like at your club.

You've now bounced a few ideas around in terms of potential initiatives that will help you achieve the goal(s) that you identified. These initiatives will help you to get closer to what you want to achieve and, importantly, will engage new or existing fans and get them excited about coming to your stadium and getting behind the team.

CAPTIVATE

TAKEAWAY TASK: Your mini audit

Now it's your turn to complete a mini audit. Here are some questions to help you get started:
- Who are you going to involve?
- What are 2-4 initiatives you think will be the most beneficial for the club?
- How will you know if the initiative is successful?

FOUR
Cutting-Edge Tech

In the previous chapter, I said that you may not have to use technology to implement a campaign or improvement, and that's absolutely true. It's also true that in most cases the correct and appropriate use of technology can make your life a lot easier. In this chapter, I'm going to explain how technology can help you.

The thing you need to understand is that when it comes to technology, it's only going to be effective if you know what you want the outcome to be. Making guesses with technology is a risky and expensive strategy and will frustrate you, your staff and your fans. It will make you feel that you're not making any progress, and over time everyone will lose faith in any potential for technology to be transformational at your club.

Once you're clear on what you want to achieve, doing an audit of your current technology situation is a good thing. You might uncover abilities or features in your existing systems that you didn't realise you had access to. Equally, you may find that things have been left for a little too long and the technology that is supposed to be supporting you day to day has become a little outdated or stagnant.

The landscape is changing

The exciting thing is that you're alive during a time when technology is the most powerful it has ever been and developing at a faster rate than ever before. We have seen incredible advances over the last couple of decades. The speed of technology evolution will only get faster and that can only mean positive things for you and your club.

As technology improves and becomes more efficient, it also becomes more affordable and accessible. If in the past you have not explored certain solutions because of the cost, I'm confident that you will now be able to find something that is affordable and brings a level of improvement to your operation as well.

It was exactly because of these developments in technology that I was able to start my company. If I had decided to start Kaizen in 1999, the sheer cost would have probably been enough for me to realise I couldn't.

CUTTING-EDGE TECH

I would have faced the costs of hosting and maintaining servers and running offices to house teams of people to build the product and maintain the infrastructure, and I would then have had to recruit even more staff to take care of things like ticket fulfilment and call centre operations. That's before I even looked at all the things I didn't know I didn't know – both technical and just the things that no one tells you about starting or running a business. It would have been an even greater expense to hire more staff or consultants or buy the right textbooks.

When I got started in 2014, I could rely on cloud services to take care of server hosting and infrastructure. I could leverage the freelance market to hire in the right skills as and when I needed them. Because of the advances in messaging and video-calling tools, a team could be located anywhere in the world. It meant people were no longer restricted by geography – the best skilled person available for the job was accessible at the time you needed them. Delivery methods like e-tickets and habits like buying online or on a phone were on the rise, so call centres and fulfilment departments were no longer a must-have. Filling in my knowledge gaps could be done with the information available online through a Google search or via online courses and in-person coding workshops and boot camps – I benefited from a few of those.

The point I'm making is that the way we do things is always changing. We're seeing a new wave of change with AI, and machine learning tools are now becoming mainstream. To fill in knowledge gaps today, you might ask ChatGPT rather than search Google. Over time, other emerging technologies like blockchain will find their place and we might be able to use them to save ourselves even more time and money. I'm laying all of this out for you to get you thinking about what time-consuming, outdated and manual tasks you can look to eliminate with better use of emerging technology.

Embrace these exciting times. I bet that in another ten years, we'll probably be laughing that we had to scan a ticket to get into a football ground as we casually let the turnstile reader scan our retinas to gain entry.

What if you're not comfortable with tech?

Now, the last few paragraphs may have scared you a bit. I know that often even thinking about having to adapt to new technologies and changing how you've done something for many years may make you feel uncomfortable. That's perfectly normal – change is hard and can often come with new challenges. My one plea to you is to not rule it out just yet. Later on in this chapter, we'll look at a case study that illustrates how clubs of any size can benefit from embracing technology.

I appreciate there might be divided opinion about the best use of technology at your club. Depending on the time and budget you have available, you may feel like your only option is to continue with the things you know and have been doing for years, maybe even decades. My example earlier of how I started my company will help you to see that it's possible to do a lot with so little these days. By staying positive and open-minded, you'll soon be starting to think, *I'm up for giving it a try, how do I get started?*

That's a great attitude and an excellent question. Let me share some thoughts with you on that.

Ensuring buy-in

In my experience, the first and most important place to start from is buy-in. If you're the only person at the club who is committed to making it work, it will be a tough gig. Rather than bringing a new technology partner on board and hoping it will all work out, I'd recommend going back over the previous two chapters of this book and ensuring you get internal alignment first. It will make the implementation process so much easier.

Computers are hard. Things won't always go to plan and if you don't have support from your colleagues or superiors, this can be quite a difficult and lonely place. Get your colleagues involved, get some buy-in at various levels, be comfortable with not getting it right the first time and agree that you're going to support each other all the way as you dive into this exciting new chapter for the club.

ALL TICKET

If you are a larger club – and by larger, I am talking about clubs with full-time staff, someone dedicated to managing ticketing as their only role and four- and five-figure attendances – then there are further considerations for you. It is likely that your technology choices will have longer-term consequences, there is the potential for upheaval, as you'll be asking fans to switch in some way, and there may be knock-on effects impacting other departments in the club.

Poor implementation of new technology can be harmful to a club. If there isn't a strong desire to change or a bad decision on the introduction of new systems has been made, it can significantly set a club back.

A 'trust the system' mentality is essential in the early stages. In many cases, you're going to be collecting and accessing data that you couldn't possibly have seen before. That data may shock you at times as you learn that your season ticket holders aren't showing up as often as you thought or you've sold more child match tickets than there were children in the ground.

The attitude towards change is the difference in these types of scenarios. The person who didn't want change in the first place will likely brush it under the carpet, tell their colleagues that it doesn't work and eventually give up.

The person who wants to make positive changes will investigate that insight a bit further. They might look for ways to increase ticket usage by running promotions or campaigns aimed at season ticket holders and incentivising them to use their tickets more often.

When you're introducing new systems or processes there will be an element of picking your battles. You can rarely implement everything you want all at once, so prioritising and delivering iteratively is a sensible way to get up and running. Sorry to say it, but debating with a ticketing or commercial manager who is obsessing over 'number of clicks' makes me die a little inside every time I have to do it... *Everyone* knows this is an outdated metric, and clarity for your user at each step is the more valuable measure... I know you agree, right?

Having the right people

To make this work, you have to have the right people involved. The success of a new implementation is always dependent on people's attitudes towards change. It is important to think about who is making the decisions. My biggest piece of advice to you is to avoid non-tech people making technical decisions. What do I mean by 'non-tech'? Someone who doesn't have some experience of working in the software industry, on software products or with a range of vendors.

You may need to work with a technology consultant for a few months to help you get on track. Like in any profession, there are good ones and bad ones, so if you're looking around, ask about their experience of working with other football clubs, request to see examples of previous projects that are similar to yours, and, ideally, speak to a few of their previous clients who have seen a project through end to end.

The downside of having someone who doesn't have the right technical experience driving these kinds of projects is that you'll spend far too much time focussing on the wrong things.

Technical confidence can play a key role, but it is not essential. I have seen many people who by their own admission aren't 'good on computers' take on a new system and run with it – simply because they want to make a change for the better at their club. They're prepared to spend a bit of time learning what they need to know and then enthusiastically use their new systems to drive improvements and efficiencies throughout various areas of the club. When you look at how far their clubs have come over a twelve- to twenty-four-month period, it really is night and day.

What will have the biggest impact?

You've got the buy-in, and you've got the right person or people around you to help with your decision-making and implementation. The next, and most crucial, decision is figuring out where technology can help you the most.

It could be with the fundamentals – things such as your club website, selling tickets or merchandise sales. It may be an improvement to your turnstiles and ticket scanning, digital signage, a new club app or something more advanced like integrations with email marketing tools, CRM systems or other membership systems.

If you have been through the exercises in the previous two chapters, you'll have a strong idea of where the priority is for you, so this decision shouldn't seem particularly overwhelming. If you were to jump straight into this part without doing any of the previous work, it would feel like you've got a lot of choices without knowing where to start. This way, you can shut out some of the noise and avoid getting too distracted by the shiny new tools and possibilities. When you've got an aim and know your priorities, you can focus on the technology that helps you to improve in that area first.

If this is still sounding a bit daunting for you, let me introduce you to someone who has walked this path already, with the arguably harder task of making a successful transition further down the football pyramid, where both money and time is tight.

CASE STUDY: A digital transformation

Chris Newbold is the fixtures secretary at Hitchin Town – a non-league football club in Hertfordshire. Due to the limited number of people available to manage day-to-day operations at the club, Chris also manages the club ticketing and merchandise system that Kaizen supplies.

Chris said, 'We had a big FA Cup match in our first season using Kaizen and decided to make the game all ticket. This was a big eye-opener for us at the club as we started to understand all the different ways the system could help us for both online and face-to-face sales.

'Like many clubs, the real catalyst for change was the pandemic. The software became a critical tool in the management of our day-to-day operations. From track and trace to managing limited inventory, we used the technology to synchronise movement around the ground.'

He added, 'The more we pushed online sales, the more we noticed the demographic changing at matches. We saw more younger people and families in addition to the previous over-fifty crowd. After our rebrand in 2021, we really pushed an online-only merchandise range, and we controversially continued to force advanced purchase online even after the COVID restrictions were removed. We invested in the infrastructure around the club, improving the Wi-Fi and building a small box office.

'Five years on, we find that 80% of our supporters buy in advance online and we still don't accept cash at the turnstiles. We're now able to forecast better and make accurate predictions on attendances.'

Chris puts the success of the digital transformation at the club down to two key areas. 'Reliable internet at the ground is important,' he says. 'Going cashless has changed everything for us. Cash causes queues! Banks are closing, so depositing it isn't easy and we're protecting our volunteers by not putting them in potentially dangerous or tempting situations.'

Seeing how a club like Hitchin has embraced technology to improve the experience of their supporters at the ground is inspiring. It's a reminder that so much can be achieved with focus in the right areas and it's possible without a huge budget.

Technology is a leveller

You're beginning now to see how technology, if used correctly, can level the playing field. You don't need to be a computer whizz to get the most out of it, and with some thought and deliberate application, it will assist you in doing the basics well. If you do the basics well, you will have solid foundations to build on and you will have earned the luxury to make a choice on what area you want to optimise next.

I've seen technology level the playing field at so many clubs during the last ten years. At Kaizen, in addition to helping over 100 non-league football clubs sell their first ever e-ticket, we were enabling many of these clubs to sell mobile tickets long before teams much higher up the leagues did. We have volunteers acting as their ticket office managers – setting up matches from their mobile phones while sitting at home on the sofa, or looking at the latest number of scanned entries from their phone while standing in a terrace on match day. I know ticketing managers at clubs in the professional ranks that still can't do that. The size of the stadium or complexity of sales shouldn't be a factor. The technology is available to everyone. Your goal is to make sure that your club is taking advantage of what is readily available to you.

Remember that the technology will help you collect data and insights, but that is only the start. The real work is interpreting that insight and coming up with a plan to improve or capitalise on a situation. That is where your ticketing strategy comes in, and we'll get into some of those details in the second part of this book.

Tips to get you started

To summarise the issues around good and bad implementations of new technology or systems, here are my top three tips on things to watch out for:

1. **Be clear on what the club wants to achieve with this new technology.** Use the previous two chapters as a guide to get you to a point where you can articulate what you want the outcome to be. Can you decide on what you will measure that will tell you if success has been achieved?

2. **Make sure everyone is well trained before they have to use it in a live scenario.** Learning anything new is hard. Learning it while trying to deal with a queue of people desperately trying to get in to see the start of a match is stressful. Prioritise training to make sure everyone is as comfortable as they can be.

3. **Clear and consistent communication makes all the difference.** Internally and externally, make sure everyone affected by the change or the introduction of new systems knows how it will impact them and what is required from them and when.

And a bonus one to help you get the best out of your suppliers:

4. **Become great at articulating the problem you want them to solve for you or the end result you're hoping they will help you to achieve –** but *don't* tell them how to fix your problem.

This might seem controversial, so I'm going to unpack it a bit.

A technology supplier who you appoint is (hopefully) an expert in their field. They might even work with other customers who have experienced similar problems to you. They will have a broader sense of what is feasible with their products and perhaps be able to see a solution that works for you and is beyond what you believed to be possible. Even better, they might have experience of doing the same thing multiple times elsewhere. You can benefit from what they learned each time they delivered a solution for someone else.

The best thing you can bring to the conversation with them is context and a list of the must-haves – the things that matter to your fans, your staff or the club in general. Give them as much context as possible about your world: the conditions you work in, the equipment you use, the skill set of your staff, the infrastructure at the club and so on.

Let them present your options back to you. You'll be amazed at how much easier it will make things. Remember, you don't know what you don't know. There's no pressure on you to have the answers – that is what you're bringing your suppliers in for. Choose them wisely and they will do all the heavy lifting for you.

A word on integrations

One final area to touch on is integrations. They can be a great way to create a tech ecosystem around your club. Having multiple systems sharing relevant data can be a powerful tool for you. The best saying I can share with you on this is 'Just because you can doesn't mean you should.'

Despite what some may lead you to believe, integrations aren't always easy. The part that no one ever talks to you about (particularly when they're selling you the dream) is the ongoing maintenance required to make sure data is being shared accurately and safely and the responsibility for service and support once the integration is up and running. If you hear salespeople churning out phrases such as 'just a snippet of JavaScript', 'open API' or 'just plugs in seamlessly' when they're selling you the dream, turn and run – and don't look back. Of course, I hope you can detect a hint of sarcasm in this, but the reality is that no matter how easy or simple people tell you an integration is, it rarely is. Integrations are unique and, unfortunately, things seldom just plug in and work.

Integration requires two parties to work together and to take responsibility for their role in support and maintenance after the work is done. As the customer in this scenario, make sure you're content that those two parties are compatible. Make sure they're clear about where the responsibilities lie and you're confident that they will be able to support you after the work is done. Please remember that they're working with your data. Treat that like gold. Question them about their security practices and approach to some of the challenges you may face with GDPR. Think of some things that could go wrong and ask who you should contact in the event of those scenarios. Do it when both parties are in the same room with you and see what answers you get. That will give you a good indication of compatibility.

The worst thing you can do in this situation is leave two parties to 'get on with it' and assume they'll just work it out. As much as it's their responsibility to support you, it is yours to make sure they play nicely together.

In most cases, the integrations that look the most effortless are the ones that have required a lot of work under the hood that you don't see. My final and most important tip in this area is to make sure you are overly clear about what you want the integration to do. If you don't know why you're connecting two systems, the supplier of each probably won't either. We have a list of questions that we share with our clients who are seriously considering an integration with our product, called The Starting Eleven. We won't proceed with any development work until there are clear and detailed answers to all eleven questions. We'll work through them with our customers and by doing that, we can all be sure what we're expecting to happen, with no assumptions or surprises. I've shared those questions with you in the accompanying resource pack – I hope they're as useful for you as they have been for us over the years. They've prevented a lot of wasted development hours, frustrated clients and assumed outcomes.

Depending on your comfort level with technology, and if this is a big shift for your club, I appreciate that this chapter might feel a bit overwhelming – and that is OK. It can often feel like there is so much to consider and it is impossible to pick where to start. The key is to just start. As you get moving, the most important areas that need your attention will soon become apparent.

CUTTING-EDGE TECH

What I can guarantee is that embracing technology will make your role easier over the long term. It isn't there to replace you, despite what you might read from some on social media. Your football club's heritage and tradition has lasted for more than 100 years in most cases. That isn't going to change any time soon. We'll all be long gone before there is any hint of the robots taking over. Think of your technology as a capable assistant that should take a lot of the manual element of your work away. It will free you up to think more strategically and let you focus on the fun stuff.

As we wrap up this chapter, I have another question for you.

We've talked about the considerations around your technology choices. Everyone who reads this will be at a different stage of their journey with technology, but I'd love for you to consider what barriers you may have to overcome as you look to introduce or overhaul the technology at your club.

TAKEAWAY TASK: Overcoming barriers

List three potential barriers that you'll face and some ideas for overcoming them. You'll have found a bit of inspiration from the previous chapters and examples shared so far.

FIVE
Communication

Most of the problems that we see between a club and its fans could be solved with better communication. We know that supporters often complain that they haven't felt listened to, and not just by their club, but in many cases the wider authorities too. A poll of 2,000 adults who attend football matches, carried out in October 2024 by Fireball Whisky in the UK, revealed that 67% reported increasingly feeling like an 'afterthought' from football's authorities.[2]

While it's pretty much impossible to get everyone to agree on every decision that is made, making the

---

2. R Jenkins, 'Football fans feel like an afterthought and want changes to be made to improve experiences', *Express* (3 October 2024), www.express.co.uk/sport/football/1956893/salford-city-football-club-fans, accessed 1 May 2025

ALL TICKET

effort to consult with fans can go a long way, even if they don't always get the outcome they're hoping for. We're going to dive into communication with fans in this chapter.

In fairness, this is an area that so many clubs have worked hard to improve in recent years and it's not uncommon now for clubs to set up regular, in-person fan forums and steering groups or even have fan representatives at senior-level meetings to make sure that the opinions of the fans are being heard and considered. This goes up a level when you have a club that is fan-owned.

Some fans will tell you that they've had a rough ride in years gone by: the price of supporting their team has continued to rise year after year, but they still show up week after week, through thick and thin, come rain or shine. Given the commitment and support they give their club season after season, it's understandable that they feel like they should receive regular and open communication from the club in return.

From what I've seen, supporters tend to not react too positively when things are sprung on them. No warning, no consultation – just implemented and they are expected to get on with it. We see it most seasons with things like pricing changes, moving season ticket holders to another section of the ground, brand and badge updates or even seemingly simple things like a change of catering suppliers on match day. Some football supporters are creatures of habit. If you're going to change things around them, they want to know and have time to prepare for it.

Building on what we've covered so far, communication has been a key part of our methodology when helping clubs to transform. It can feel like a lot of rapid change in some cases, so it's more important than ever to make sure a club is set up to bring the fans on that journey with them, to maximise the chances of success and to make the transition a smooth one.

The first question I have for you is 'How is your club keeping the fans updated at the moment?' You're going to need to make sure you have a solid communication plan as you begin to implement new ideas and new systems. If you don't have the means to make frequent updates, you'll need to think about how you can change that too. We're going to explore some ideas throughout this chapter and look at some tactics in the second part of the book.

Fan engagement is a thing

Like many new trends, fan engagement became a bit of a buzzword for a while. Everyone was apparently doing it, but no one could articulate what exactly they were doing that they hadn't already been doing. Things have moved on a bit now and it's great to see clubs appointing individuals or organisations to give this some real thought and in many cases develop a strategy around it.

By now, you'll be joining the dots already. Your approach to fan engagement is a critical part of your ticketing strategy. Making sure people have the best time when they visit you is what makes them want to come back again and again. It is what creates trust from new fans and encourages people to spread the word about what a great time they have whenever they come to your club. Don't forget that this isn't limited to match days and it's definitely not limited to what happens inside the ground.

Football clubs have had to work harder than ever to attract and retain fans, as people now have more choice when it comes to how they're going to spend their hard-earned money on a Saturday afternoon or Tuesday evening. That might be an individual looking for something to do or a parent looking for ideas to keep their kids entertained.

For far too long, clubs relied on loyalty, and for some it almost became an excuse to stop trying. 'The fans are not going to go and watch another team' became a belief that was too common at a lot of clubs. That belief evolved into serving substandard food at matches, not maintaining the toilets or letting the terraces fall into disrepair. While many fans grumbled and got on with it, others found something else to spend their money on. The casual fans decided to go and watch another sport or spend their money on a night out instead. The parents opted for swimming, the cinema or bowling on a Saturday afternoon. Like a slow, painful death, the clubs that had neglected the fan experience started to see a decline in crowds. No matter how many 'kids for a quid' offers they did, it just didn't seem to make a noticeable difference.

I've told many clubs over the years that their competition isn't each other – off the pitch at least. The real competition is the leisure centre down the road or the soft play centre or bowling alley. Parents generally have a budget when it comes to entertaining their children and they also have choice – more choice than ever these days.

Luckily, most clubs are well aware of that now and have made great progress in making their grounds more inviting. In the last five years or so, going to watch football outside of the top flight has become more of an attractive option for many. It's usually affordable for parents who have to consider admission, food, a visit to the club shop etc. The atmosphere is generally better for those that like a sing-song and the general feeling of community hasn't been lost, as some would argue has happened with some of the top-flight grounds these days. If anything, community has never been stronger, particularly at non-league grounds. Being able to speak to the manager in the bar afterwards and kids being able to grab a selfie with their favourite player are simple acts that go a long way with supporters and make them feel valued.

Fan engagement is about doing all these things and more. It is about everything from working out how much people are going to have to spend and how appealing the ground is to visit, to what options they have to eat and drink when they're there, how welcoming the atmosphere is and, overall, how much of a reason you give them to come back and do it all again next time. Ticketing, and your communication strategy around it, plays an important role in that experience.

Communicating with the fans

In the previous chapter, we took a deep dive into our options around technology. One of the technology choices you may have to make is what is the best tool for the job when it comes to communicating with the fans.

You are going to need ways of letting them know about some of the amazing new offers and campaigns you have created for them after going through our Clarity and Captivate chapters. I hope you're so excited about them, you can't wait to share that with the fans and, in turn, get them excited about spending money with the club and coming to support the team.

You can go down the route of old-fashioned, offline approaches. Leaflets, posters, word of mouth – they all have a place and shouldn't be overlooked. You've got to meet people where they are with this one. This is a phrase I use a lot, but I stand by it. There's no point in relying on push notifications from your shiny new app if most of your fans haven't downloaded it because they don't want another app on their phone. That said, is this an area where you can leverage technology and start to spread the word?

There's no doubt digital communication will help you to get the word out at scale. You can give frequent updates with minimal cost and effort digitally. Once you get into a rhythm and develop some consistency in terms of how frequently you communicate with fans, it becomes a simple, repeatable and manageable process.

Let's take a look at some common approaches and quick wins when it comes to developing communication with the fans. If you've been doing nothing at all in this area up to now, don't feel like you have to do all of these at once. In fact, please *don't* do all of these at once. The fans will appreciate some form of communication from the club, but you run the risk of overkill if you do too much too soon, and then everyone switches off.

Newsletters

This is the most basic and simple approach there is. You're collecting email addresses and marketing preference information when fans transact with you – remember that digital marketing is your friend. You have the data already, so it should be easy for you to send a newsletter to anyone who has opted in to receiving marketing communications from the club. If you're not sure what people have opted in to receiving, I'd recommend getting some specialist advice around GDPR, just to make sure you're staying compliant.

You can start off by being generic with your newsletter content. I've shared some template ideas with you in the bonus materials. As you get a bit more confident with your emailing software, you can (and should) start to segment your audience a bit more. This is just a fancy way of saying 'send relevant stuff to the right people'. You can develop a more structured newsletter with reminders of upcoming sale periods and away matches, and other ticket office news like travel options, match bundles or offers can be a great way to keep your club in the mind of your supporters. Achieving consistency is difficult, but is key to making this work.

When it comes to using your newsletter for pushing ticket sales or promotions, there are some quick wins you can use with the data that you will have collected from your ticketing system. Here are three simple fan segments to consider for email newsletter offers:

1. Season tickets

    – Anyone who doesn't have a season ticket but has purchased tickets for more than seven matches

    – Anyone who had a season ticket earlier than last season but hasn't bought for the current season

2. Match tickets

    - Anyone who is a first-time purchaser – invite them back with an offer (second ticket half price, kid for a quid etc)
    - Anyone who hasn't purchased a ticket for more than three months – send them a 'Where have you been? We've missed you' email

3. Hospitality

    - Supporters with an upcoming birthday in the next two months – invite them to upgrade to a hospitality ticket or give them an offer in your hospitality areas

Online forums

These always make me smile, as I think this was the original birthplace of the keyboard warrior. Forums have been around since the dawn of the internet and looking at many of them today, they've not been updated since then – but don't overlook the valuable information that you can find in these places. Ironically, it always seems the best ones are independently run, so if you can create an engaged, club-run forum, you're onto a winner. If not, tap into the existing independent ones. This is where you'll hear all kinds of opposing views from your supporters. It's a great place to get a temperature check on fan sentiment. While useful, I'd always put a caveat on these, though. They're not always representative of the entire supporter base, so I'd always cross-check what I find with another reference point. From the club's point of view, a forum is a great tool to push messages and ideas out to fans at scale and get feedback quickly.

In-person events

Forums, Q&A sessions, 'meet the manager' events and engagement groups are a fantastic way to bring supporters together with the opportunity to visit the club on a non-match day. It gives them a chance to feel like they're going behind the scenes a little and to hear the latest club news, directly from a club official or the manager. Making these as much of a two-way interaction as possible is key. When supporters feel like they have the chance to ask questions and provide their opinions and feedback, they're usually happy. It could be an idea to moderate questions ahead of time to avoid embarrassing situations or just to avoid labouring a minor detail for too long during the event. Whether it's in-person or online meetings, many clubs meet with selected fans to give updates on ticketing initiatives and get feedback from fans on what is working or needs improvement.

Regular surveys

Some clubs look for ongoing feedback from fans through surveys, which they make accessible after each match, or email to supporters after they've been to a match to get their thoughts on facilities, accessibility, ease of buying a ticket etc. We will look at these in detail in Chapter Eight.

Monthly briefing from a senior club official

Supporters love to hear from someone at the club and feel like they're getting inside information. Things like monthly open letters as well as short articles in the club programme to let supporters know the latest thinking from the club are always popular.

Social media

Think of ways you can use social media and have dedicated ticket office accounts. Obviously, this will need a lot of attention, and rapid response is crucial to making this work. If you have a team of people looking after this account, it becomes much easier. I would only recommend this if you're set up to respond to queries quickly. If you're a ticket office of one, you don't need this added to your workload.

Don't forget your international fans

This is an area that often gets overlooked. If they're outside of the top flight, many clubs simply assume that there isn't much of an international interest in them.

How wrong they have been. Just because your club may not have hundreds of thousands or even millions of followers across your social media channels doesn't mean that people outside of the local community aren't also interested in what you're up to or how the team are doing.

We first discovered this accidentally when we helped a few non-league clubs to offer merchandise sales alongside their tickets online. Within the first few weeks, orders were coming in from all over the world: Hitchin Town fans in Australia, King's Lynn Town fans in Canada – you wouldn't believe it.

Back in 2018, indie rock band The Libertines decided to sponsor Margate FC. The band's logo would appear on the front of both the home and away shirt as part of the deal. This opened up a completely new segment of fans for the club. Libertines fans from all over the world needed to get their hands on a Margate shirt and when they went on sale, we found ourselves helping the club to sell shirts worldwide. Shirts were sold to Libertines fans in over sixty-one countries. Many in turn became fans of the club through the band's association and have either made an effort to visit for a match or buy season and match tickets as a way of donating money to the club. Six years later, the partnership is still going strong and the club has benefited from a growing international audience as a result.

You may not have a world-famous band ready to step in and sponsor your club, but I guarantee that you will have fans who have moved away from the area or are living abroad and still keeping an eye out for your results – and would probably like a way of staying involved with the club somehow. Don't overlook your international audience – find them and keep in touch. We'll look at a few other ways you can do this and another great example from a club we've worked with in the second part of the book as we put the focus on creating your own strategy.

Communicating with overlooked groups

You can and should be communicating with overlooked groups; for example, local businesses, schools, junior football clubs and charities can be accidentally ignored by clubs. I'm talking about more than just the transactional relationship of 'Buy an advertising board and then we'll never speak again until it's time to renew.' From a ticketing perspective, there are so many more opportunities to work with and involve local small business owners and help each other thrive in the process.

Going back to a key principle of the earlier chapters, I'm going to ask that annoying question again: 'What do you want to focus on?' Getting more people into the stadium or getting the people who are already there to spend more money?

If you're focussing on getting more people in, then why not give tickets to local businesses as part of your outreach? They are part of the community. In many cases, their own businesses will do better if there are more people coming to your stadium, so for some there will be a genuine interest in seeing the club do well. This relationship should be more than a transactional one, where they're buying minor sponsorship. While that is one way of working with them, I'm going to encourage you to think more broadly and play a longer-term game with them. Many of these businesses have something that is valuable to your club: access to local people, whether that is a database of people in the area that they can market to, real estate in prime areas of your community or a social media following that extends further than your own. As a forward-thinking club, look for ways you can help each other and use each other's assets for mutual benefit.

We'll get into some tactics to develop these thoughts further in the second part of the book. I want to challenge you to think about ways you can collaborate with the business community to help you sell more tickets and bring new people into the club. You both have something the other party wants – that's the perfect recipe for a great partnership.

To finish up this chapter, I am going to give you a simple takeaway task on the subject of using local businesses to help you sell more tickets. Some may argue that this isn't strictly the job of the ticketing manager, but remember: you should be thinking bigger than just looking after your area at the club. If this means collaborating with a commercial manager or whoever looks after partnerships at the club, do it. I'm sure they'll be grateful for the assistance and fresh ideas.

> **TAKEAWAY TASK: Involving local businesses**
>
> Can you come up with three ways you could involve a local business with the club, which would be of value for them and, in turn, would help you to attract a new group of supporters to the club? Think about what they might have that is useful to you. Previously, I mentioned their location and a database, or it could be a reputation or an association.

SIX
Confidence

In this chapter, I'll introduce you to the final C of our five C's. This is where I'll help you start to build your confidence. By now, you'll have a plan, you'll be better aligned with your colleagues, and you'll even have some offers and campaigns lined up to help you get closer to achieving the plan that you are all committed to delivering.

You have audited your technology and introduced or upgraded some systems. You now also have a clear process for telling your supporters what is happening and when. Your improved line of communication means no one will be able to moan about being kept in the dark any more. Things are suddenly looking much better.

That leaves us with the last and most important step to work on – you.

Working on yourself

Going through everything I've just mentioned will be hard work, but at the same time it will result in you having a greater sense of control over your day-to-day. By eliminating the noise and having a clear focus, you will simplify your working day as you develop a sense of what is important for now and what can be set aside for later. It's at this point that you'll probably feel that, for the first time in a long time, you can start to think about planning longer-term ideas, rather than firefighting every day.

This is where you give yourself the space to be able to think about ticketing on a strategic level – something you probably didn't ever think you'd have the time to do previously, because there was always something urgent to deal with first. This is where you now have the time and the headspace to start looking carefully at the many hats you've been wearing in your role and work out what you're comfortable with and where you need a bit of extra support.

I mentioned at the beginning of the book that your role is a generalist one. I don't know many people responsible for ticketing who have undergone any kind of formal training for this job, simply because it has never existed. The closest alternative I have seen is ticketing managers supporting each other in fragmented, DIY WhatsApp groups or during a chance meeting

CONFIDENCE

in person at a random industry event, where a few war stories are shared and words of encouragement exchanged.

That is something I've often toyed with the idea of addressing by setting up an independent ticketing manager group where anything goes and it doesn't matter what system you use, what level your club is playing at or how long you've been in the job. A place where any rivalries are put to one side and where a group of like-minded people, all trying to do the same job, can get together to share best practices. Somewhere for the newer and inexperienced folks to fast-track their progress and for the older, more experienced operators to share good practice.

I've set up a Facebook group with exactly this in mind. Search Facebook for 'All Ticket Community' and join us.

Working through the season

One thing that won't change is the number of things there are to do throughout the season. You are still going to have multiple matches to prepare for at the same time. What I would hope for you by now, though, is that you'll have the capacity to be able to deal with those matches without three other emergencies cropping up as you're trying to get on with something that requires your full concentration.

ALL TICKET

By now, the senior management at the club will have a better understanding of what you have to deal with as the ticketing manager. If you've actively involved them in the earlier process of defining some strategic ticketing objectives, it will happen naturally. You might find that you've been able to get additional help in the form of an extra staff member or general improvements to the working conditions and infrastructure that was discussed in earlier chapters.

If that's the case, now is the time to make the best use of it. This is where you can start to organise a ticket office team to support you. Encourage more ownership and responsibility, build up the roles of your team members and create even more space for you to be able to manage the operation and not get so bogged down in fiddly day-to-day issues.

Most ticket offices that I've known in this position have split responsibilities between people depending on the size of the club. It doesn't mean that any one person stops doing a particular job, but that one person now takes ownership of it with everyone else supporting as much or as little as needed. You will start to shift away from feeling like everything is down to you alone. Of course, this doesn't mean certain things aren't your problem anymore – if you're in charge of ticketing, you're still ultimately responsible for that, but you're now encouraging your team to take on some of that responsibility to help to free you up to plan for the future and make your operation even more efficient.

CONFIDENCE

If you are a ticket office of one, this is obviously going to be a bit harder, but, now that you have gone through the process so far, I would expect you to feel a better sense of control and, ultimately, things should feel a little less chaotic. Perhaps now is the time to make the case for some assistance in the ticket office. If the club is serious about improving ticketing, you're going to need some day-to-day support putting those plans into action. Either way, I salute you if it's just you – it's not easy.

Don't be a hero

A phrase I have heard throughout my career and now use myself is 'don't be a hero'. In that fast-paced ticket office environment, it is easy to get caught up trying to do two or three things at once. I would even go as far as to say some people thrive off it. I used to include myself in that group, until I learned the ultimate lesson in why it is not an approach that will serve you well in the long run.

Let me take you back to 2008. It was another busy day in our luxury Portakabin. We had a team of fourteen at the time, so on the face of it you would think there were more than enough people to take care of everything that needed to be done. I guess it's all relative. Even with a team of that size, it felt like there was a never-ending list of things to do throughout the season.

ALL TICKET

On this particular day, we were a couple of staff members short, so I found myself multitasking a bit more than usual – hopping on the phone when it got busy and jumping on the counter to help if there was a small queue forming. My priority for the day was to get two lots of away allocations out to clubs that would be visiting in the next couple of months. We used to categorise matches based on perceived demand, so I had to print 3,000 tickets for a category B match and another 3,000 for a category A match, which happened to be a local derby. I would have to remember to change the prices on the ticket manually in between printing them for one game and the next.

Long story short, I got distracted and after printing the category B tickets, I forgot to change the price and printed all the category A's at the much cheaper category B price. I didn't check them and shipped them off to the visiting teams.

It wasn't picked up until a couple of weeks later. I got a phone call one Sunday morning from a colleague to let me know that *The Mail on Sunday* had run a story about the printing mistake and it was in the paper that day. I can't even begin to describe the feeling. You want to be sick, cry and swear all at once.

Going into work the next day was grim. In fairness, everyone was pretty understanding. I didn't get the sack and we managed to recover most of the deficit with a lot of help from our colleagues in the visiting team's ticket office – but it still haunts me to this day.

CONFIDENCE

I sometimes joke that you haven't really made it in our industry until you've been involved in a situation labelled as a shambles, fiasco or farce, and this was mine. The article is still online now, so if you want to see the full story, I'm sure you'll be able to find it with a bit of googling.

Because I'm a glutton for punishment, I go back and look at the article from time to time, particularly when I find myself feeling like I'm trying to do too many things at once. It's my way of reminding myself that I need to slow down. You'll pay for it later one way or another. Don't be a hero.

To bring you back to the modern day, I was at an event a couple of weeks ago during the time when I was writing this chapter. The ticket office manager from the visiting team was also there. I hadn't seen him for at least fifteen years. Within ten minutes of us catching up, he asked me, 'Do you remember that time when…?' These things will follow you forever.

If something like that happens to you, just own it. Do your best to rectify it and, even better, use my mistake to learn the lesson: slow down, take a breath and don't try to be the hero.

Prepare for Manchester City every week

I guarantee that once you have worked through the five C's process, you will feel much more confident when it comes to your ticketing operation. Don't rush through it. Revisit parts if necessary. Remember that it is hard to guess everything correctly up front, so there's nothing wrong with a change of direction if the data tells you that might be a good idea. When we do this with clubs that we work with, it can sometimes take a couple of seasons to solidify. When you set up certain campaigns, they might not fly straight away, but I want you to understand that you don't have to be right every time. It's a learning process and mistakes are par for the course.

Remember how in Chapter Two I talked about approaching this like an experiment? Sometimes, experiments fail and that will be no different when you start to implement some of the ideas we have explored so far. The key is to make sure you get to that point as quickly and cheaply as possible and to make sure there has been something to learn on the way. You can use that learning to your advantage as you go into your next experiment.

In Chapter Two I encouraged you to think of some of these initiatives as mini campaigns. Again, don't worry if they're not all game changers when you first start. There will be plenty to take away from the work that has been done over a short cycle, which will inform the next campaign and help you to figure out what works best for the club and, importantly, for your supporters.

CONFIDENCE

Now you have a plan, you will naturally feel more confident in your role. The reactive tasks will be fewer and fewer. You will confidently be able to categorise what work is absolutely necessary versus things that are a distraction. You can rely on the support of your colleagues in other areas of the club, as you've aligned on the outcomes you're all focussed on.

In Chapter Four I talked about the importance of a 'trust the system' mentality. When you've audited your technology and you know you're working with software that is giving you accurate data that you can do something with, you will make decisions with renewed confidence.

Trusting the system isn't just about technology, though. As you go through the steps outlined in the book and start to see a clear direction for where you want to be, you will create new internal processes and efficiencies that will help you get there, and you will develop ways to repeat them easily in the future.

Something that I always say to clubs is 'Plan your operations like you're playing Manchester City in The FA Cup third round. Then repeat that every week.' That might sound like overkill, but hear me out...

You want to get into the habit of having boring match days. Match days where the same thing happens every time you're playing at home. Boring, predictable and

ALL TICKET

repeatable. Everyone knows their role and can do it on autopilot. No surprises and nothing that you haven't seen or dealt with before. That's when you know you've cracked it and you've got a well-oiled machine. If you've prepared well in the week leading up to it, you can guarantee a boring match day for yourself.

Manchester City comes into it because we're thinking about standards. Naturally, when a team from the top of the pyramid comes to visit in a high-profile tie, smaller clubs can go on high alert. Suddenly, everyone wants to change how things are normally done.

I've seen it a few times over the years. I hear statements like: 'We need to do that update to our ticket design now, because the big boys are coming to town', 'We should sell tickets from a seating plan for this match, so we look the part', 'We better update the imagery on our site now because more people will be looking at it' and 'We should change the entrances that fans go through. We just never got around to it before.' These are all genuine things that have been said to me over the years as clubs have prepared for some of the biggest matches in their recent history.

Introducing something different when your stadium is going to be the busiest it has been for some time is probably the worst possible thing you can do if you want to guarantee a smooth, efficient (and boring) match day operation. That is where mistakes are made and staff don't know what they should or shouldn't be doing, as it isn't what they're used to.

CONFIDENCE

My challenge to you is this: insist on these higher standards being a normal feature for you every week. If you prepare for every match like you're hosting Manchester City, when Manchester City does come to town for that crunch cup game, it will be business as usual for you and your team. No nerves, no additional stress, just confidence in doing what you've been doing all season, confidence in your technology standing up to the task and confidence knowing that what you do works.

Challenge with confidence

Now you have improved data points because of your technology audit, and you have better feedback loops with supporters through improved communication from the club, you can act on this to continue to make things better. Another aspect of the 'trust the system' mentality is being able to look at the data you're collecting and being confident that it is correct. When you have that confidence, you can look at underperforming areas and start to bring about a positive change. Here's a good recent example of using some of those data points with clubs to be able to challenge something with confidence to try and improve a situation.

This season, we noticed that usage of season tickets has been slightly lower than previous years. Some of our clients also noticed the trend, looking at the data in the match day dashboards that they use in our software. The first win was that they were confidently able to identify that this metric seemed lower than normal, and, after doing a bit more research across clubs of a similar size or playing at the same level, we confirmed that this was a trend that everyone was seeing. Through their improved communication channels, some clubs were able to get feedback from supporters as to why they weren't using their season tickets as much. They did this through simple email campaigns and by bringing it up at fan forums or in general chit-chat with fans as they came to the ticket office.

With this information, we launched a new ticket forwarding feature that helped supporters to pass their ticket on for matches when they knew they couldn't make it. The club still got someone using the seat, and if there was a price difference, they made the extra money from the upgrade and would still benefit from the likelihood of additional spending at the bar, in the club shop etc.

Some clubs went a step further and allowed season ticket holders to donate their tickets back to the club, where they were reissued to people that don't usually get a chance to attend a match – a great example of the inclusivity that a football club can create in the local community. It's still early days, but the initial signs are showing that this strategy has improved ticket use for the clubs that have implemented it.

Developing the club with the five Cs

You can see from this tale how various components of the five Cs that we develop with a club all overlap and complement each other. For this to work, there needs to be confidence in the technology in the first place so the current situation can be challenged. Rather than jumping into a technical solution to the problem, the new strategy was validated by speaking to people. We don't ever want to lose that personal touch. We will always get the best results when we have people and technology working together, each informing and supporting the other.

With a lot of noise being made about various technologies automating everyone's jobs in the next few years, it's worth reiterating that this is a long way off in the world of ticketing. Your job will change, for sure. You'll probably find yourself needing to be a bit more tech-savvy or comfortable using new tools and technologies in the coming years. It's just another stage in the natural evolution of how we sell tickets.

A fair question that you might be asking yourself now is 'How do I become more comfortable with these new technologies?' Here are some tips to get you started and help you to build your confidence if it all feels a bit too much:

- **Start with the basics**: Build foundational knowledge first. Get to know the fundamentals before jumping into some of the more advanced concepts. Slow and steady wins the race.

- **Ask for specific training**: If there is a training budget available, don't be afraid to use it. If not, a good idea would be to speak with some of your existing suppliers to see if they can point you towards any resources or facilitate training themselves. They will need to master new technologies to keep their own products relevant.

- **Practise regularly**: Once you learn the basics, don't let your new knowledge go to waste. Set yourself mini tasks or scenarios that allow you to put your skills into practice. Consistency will build confidence.

- **Get support from your colleagues**: You may have some colleagues who are already experts. Ask to shadow them or, if they have the time, for them to pass their learnings on to you more informally.

- **Stay positive**: Making mistakes is part of the learning process, so don't beat yourself up if that happens. Remember to make sure you take away the lesson if things go wrong; each time you overcome a challenge, you're enhancing your skills.

People working with technology will always be needed. You will always need to have someone to join the dots, to interpret data and to decide what that means and where to focus next. If we can get you confident to be that person, there will be plenty of work for you in the ticketing world for years to come.

Let's round off this chapter with another takeaway task for you.

> **TAKEAWAY TASK: Learning to delegate**
>
> Think about what you're taking on day to day in your role currently. Is there more you can be passing on to other members of your team? Can you help develop them and give them a bit more ownership?
>
> What more can you do to help free yourself up to give yourself the time and space to look at ticketing at the club more strategically?

SEVEN
Your Ticketing Strategy

When I have an onboarding conversation with a football club, the strategic bit (or lack of) is, unfortunately, the most predictable. It usually happens after we've signed an agreement to work together and we're in an initial planning meeting, working out what needs to be done when so we can get started.

I'll usually ask something along the lines of 'So just at a really high level, what is your strategy for ticketing next season?' There is usually a pause of three to five seconds, which feel more like an awkward twenty seconds, when everyone looks at everyone else, hoping somebody will speak. Eventually, someone will say something along the lines of 'Well we just want to get the new system up and running first and then we were planning to see what it can do.'

I appreciate the sentiment, but this is the most backward approach to building a strategy to guarantee your ticketing success. Your whole strategy is going to be driven by what some software can (or can't) do? Sounds like a dangerous place to be, but now we're going to put that right.

From tactical to strategic

Over the next few chapters, we're going to switch gears. The first part of this book was tactical. I took you through a process we have used with clubs like yours multiple times. The steps I've shared with you will help you to get aligned with your colleagues and reduce the chaos in your day-to-day. It's now time to go up a level.

I'm now going to ask you to think longer term... We're going to expand your thinking beyond just selling tickets and start considering how ticketing links into other parts of the ecosystem around the club. We'll look at how you can turn your area into a huge revenue generator and become an essential team when it comes to guaranteeing long-term commercial growth.

Unfortunately, not having a ticketing strategy is extremely common. Far more common than I would like, but it makes sense when you think about it.

You walk into a new role, heading up the club's ticketing and maybe retail or memberships as well. You're

YOUR TICKETING STRATEGY

slammed day to day; there's barely time to have your lunch. You're working late on a Tuesday night when you have a match, then you're back in the next morning and again on a Saturday. The days when the team are away are cherished because you get away on time, and if you've got a free weekend, you want to make the most of it. Repeat that for nine months. It's then time to drink from the fire hose that is season ticket and membership renewal time and start the cycle all over again. Where on earth are you going to find the time to think about, never mind document, a long-term strategy for maximising revenue through the ticket office?

It's a pattern I've seen over and over, even with clubs that we don't supply technology to. We have a ticketing scorecard on our website. It's designed to help clubs figure out where they are and whether using our services can help them. One of the questions in that scorecard is 'Do you have a ticketing strategy that is shared and understood throughout the club?' At the time of writing, a staggering 95% of clubs that have taken part answered 'No' to that question. Just let that sink in: 95% of clubs are operating day to day, just hanging in there and waiting to see what happens next.

If you want to take the quiz, visit https://scorecard.kaizenticketing.com and see how you rank. Maybe finish this book first, create your ticketing strategy and help me get that 95% down to something more respectable.

The great news is that you now have a plan in place to reduce the chaos, so I'm confident that you'll be able to use that new-found spare time to work on your longer-term strategy. This is where you'll see your operation and the contribution that your area makes to the club move on leaps and bounds.

It's not just about the club

The secret to getting this right is to think about how everyone will benefit if you implement this well, not just the club. Think about who the club serves and what their aspirations are as part of the process. The obvious group to consider are your supporters, but don't overlook the wider local community and local businesses along with commercial partners and suppliers.

If you have a strong ethos in place and a clear strategy for how you can be of service to these groups while being a great partner in the process, you completely change the dynamic of the club and the relationship with all of those parties. You become a club that supporters want to get behind and it's easier to attract new fans in the process. The club becomes an attractive partner for local and national businesses, and you'll have suppliers queuing up wanting to work with you because of the prestige or the general 'good to work with' reputation that you've created.

I tell you this from first-hand experience – I will always actively pursue working with a club that has a bit of

YOUR TICKETING STRATEGY

a story about where they're going over the club that's just trudging along season after season. That applies at all levels too. I love to see a non-league club rising through the levels, with a plan to grow sustainably. I get just as much of a buzz from helping them go from gates of 150 to 1,500 as I do from a higher-ranking team increasing their season ticket revenue or moving fans from a pay-in-person cash culture to the majority buying online. As a supplier, if we can help a club achieve part of their plan, it gives us focus, and working together is way more interesting. The clubs that see their partners and suppliers as allies in this context are the ones that will benefit from the best deals and usually get the more positive outcomes. It rarely works when the relationship is transactional.

The first question to answer is: 'Are you only thinking about yourself (ie the club) as you start to pull together a ticketing strategy, or are you considering the outcomes that others want?' Other questions to answer as you're coming up with your initial ideas include:

- **Are you meeting people where they are?** For example, you've identified that many of your supporters are over sixty and have a preference to buy in person. Introducing an online-only buying policy and closing the ticket office during the week might be a bit much too soon. How could you ease people into it instead?
- **Is your strategy helpful and easy to understand?** I've worked with clubs that have toyed with the idea of introducing complicated pricing structures

in their stadiums when they struggle to fill the stands every week. There are simpler ways to increase revenue. Better still, let's focus on ways that will help you sell out consistently as the first priority.

- **Can you get there in stages?** Bear in mind how people will react to change, particularly supporters. If you're not telling them why it's happening, they will be resistant. If they don't buy into it, they will be resistant. If it feels aggressive, is there a way to get to where you want in stages? Can you paint the bigger picture and then bring them with you step by step?

- **Is it supporting the big vision?** Everyone loves being part of a story, and being able to sell the story of the journey that your club is on is no different. If everyone can see how a small part of the strategy fits into the bigger picture, they'll be more accepting or, better still, they will want to be part of it.

Implications and regulations

There are other things that affect a ticketing operation and that will influence the plan you put together. Among other things, you'll need to consider legal implications, compliance or league regulations, ground health and safety and, as an extension of that, any advice that has been given by the Safety Advisory Group (SAG).

As you'll have realised by now, as with getting any solid process in place, creating a ticketing strategy is something that should involve people from lots of different areas around the club and your external partners too. Their input will be invaluable. It will stop avoidable mistakes being made and your colleagues will appreciate being consulted while you're still putting a plan together.

Now let's look at some of these in a bit more detail.

Legal

There are a couple of different areas to consider around the legal aspect of your ticketing strategy. Having a handle on the basics is advisable when it comes to selling tickets for football matches, pricing, resale and, of course, touting. You don't need to be a lawyer, but it is good to have an awareness of some of the laws around ticket selling. Football matches are sometimes treated differently to other types of large events. Watch out for any special rules.

Criminal Justice and Public Order Act 1994: Section 166 of this act makes it a criminal offence to sell or dispose of a football match ticket without authorisation. The maximum penalty is a fine of up to £1,000.

Consumer Rights Act 2015: This act requires ticket sellers to provide certain information when reselling tickets, such as the original price and seat details. Part of your strategy may be combating the illegal resale or touting of tickets. In a BBC article in 2023, Reg Walker of Iridium Consultancy estimated that the black market for Premier League ticket touting is worth more than £50 million per year.[3] That number obviously decreases as you go further down the football pyramid, but you should have concerns over supporter safety when it comes to tickets being resold illegally. Not knowing who is coming into the stadium can lead to other safety issues in the ground.

Compliance

Don't overlook the importance of making sure you're being compliant in the way you're selling tickets. There are many things to be aware of here, so, again, working with your club or suppliers' legal counsel is strongly advised. You might find this a bit dry or dull, but, unfortunately, you will have a big problem if you're found breaking the rules.

You might remember the fuss that was made back in 2018 as everyone scrambled to be GDPR compliant. New regulations were being introduced and there was a lot of contradictory advice going around as we all prepared for the new way of doing things. While it is debatable whether everyone is acting in a compliant

---

3. K Falkingham, 'Premier League: Ticket touting a "significant and rising" problem', BBC (10 February 2023), www.bbc.co.uk/sport/football/64497260, accessed 1 May 2025

YOUR TICKETING STRATEGY

way, the threat of some pretty hefty fines if you're found to not be following the rules isn't a risk worth taking.

The same goes for PCI compliance for credit card sales and Buy-Now, Pay-Later disclosure rules in your marketing if you're selling anything across multiple instalments. It is not worth taking any risks in trying to sidestep these. Failing to comply can result in big fines or, at worst, conviction of a criminal offence.

A good supplier should know the rules and will help you to stay within them. This, however, is still your responsibility, so double-check everything and if you're in doubt, ask a qualified legal professional.

League and competition regulations

These will vary depending on the league or competition that the team is playing in. Some leagues have rules about the number of promotions you can run over the season. Other cup competitions have specific rules on the number of free tickets that can be distributed for those matches.

The person in the know here will be your club secretary. An experienced club secretary will know the rules inside out after years of dealing with the authorities. Even if they are new to the role, they will have access to the latest regulations across the competitions that the club is involved in, so they will still be able to find out what you need to know quickly. Things like visiting teams' allocations and guidance on safeguarding youngsters inside your stadium will fall under these regulations too, so make sure you're up to date with the latest advice from your league.

Health and safety

The club safety officer is someone you'll be in regular contact with throughout the season as a ticketing manager. This person has the thankless task of making sure that the stadium remains compliant with the latest safety standards and will meet frequently with a SAG.

The relationship between a club and its SAG is important but will vary from club to club. In some cases, it's collaborative and supportive. In others, there may have been some tension between the parties, and it can seem almost impossible to please everyone. The SAG will be made up of representatives from the local council, emergency services and senior club staff. Collectively, their responsibility is to make sure that the club is operating in accordance with the latest guidelines on spectator safety and not doing anything that might breach the safety certificate that has been awarded at the start of the season.

You might hear your safety officer reference the *Green Guide* now and then. This is the go-to safety manual for events, particularly for sports grounds. The *Green Guide*

YOUR TICKETING STRATEGY

promotes a proactive approach to safety management, regardless of legal obligations. It is written by the Sports Grounds Safety Authority, which was formerly the Football Licensing Authority.[4]

The golden rule I was originally taught and have since always followed throughout my career is 'Safety always wins in any debate.' If the safety officer says no, accept it and work with them to find an alternative that they are comfortable with.

Visitors and inspections

Linking in to all of these, you will find that the club will have various inspections taking place throughout the season, and you should be prepared for these. From the local authorities to the league, representatives can sometimes turn up unannounced to make sure that you're operating in a compliant way.

Not all of these visits will be ticketing-related. You may have someone from the local council turn up to inspect food hygiene standards in your kitchens and catering outlets, for example. When it comes to ticketing, it will often be the league or competition owner, wanting to check that the correct information is being displayed on your tickets. It will be part of a much wider inspection,

---

4. Sports Grounds Safety Authority, *The Guide to Safety at Sports Grounds* (2018), https://sgsa.org.uk/document/greenguide, accessed 1 May 2025

and often there is some advance warning. Going back to my earlier advice on boring match days, prepare for an inspection every match day. If you have set high standards and you know you're doing the right things, no one will be caught out if something like this is suddenly sprung on you without much notice.

The EFL Family Excellence Scheme

This organises awards that all member clubs can achieve each season, based on how good the experience of attending a match at the club is, particularly for families. Some of the areas that the scheme ranks a club on are ticket purchasing, match day entertainment, accessibility, facilities, website, social media and communications. Depending on how well a club does, it is possible to achieve gold, silver or bronze status.

Many clubs in the EFL will use the Family Excellence Scheme criteria as a cornerstone of their fan engagement strategy. What is particularly good about this is that clubs receive detailed feedback and suggestions for improvement from the league assessor as well, so there is always clear direction on which areas are working well and what could be improved.

The scheme has been running for almost twenty years. Independent assessors visit the club to carry out a 'mystery shopper' style assessment on two separate occasions in the season. They complete reports on the areas that the awards are graded on, which are then ranked and fed back to the club. There is no warning or indication as to when the assessors will visit the club, which minimises any special treatment being given. This adds more weight to the 'prepare for Manchester City every week' approach I advocated in the previous chapter. If your standards are high and it's just what you do, achieving the top mark will never be in doubt.

The Family Excellence Scheme is taken seriously by many of the clubs in the EFL and its impact was recognised recently, as it won Best Fan Engagement Programme at the 2018 Sports Business Awards.

Even if your club isn't competing in the EFL, I'd encourage you to look at the criteria and use them as a template for areas to assess your club's operations on. Having a stadium that is welcoming to families should be a priority in your fan engagement strategy. All of the touchpoints – from the first time someone contacts the club to enquire about buying a ticket through to what the experience is like on a match day and not forgetting how you continue the relationship with them after – are key areas to think about that will determine whether someone will be a one-off visitor or a regular attendee over the season.

Let's create

Over the next three chapters, I am going to share some ideas with you that will help you to shape a ticketing strategy for your club. In the additional resources, you will find some tools to help you plan the areas of the strategy you create.

The approach I will show you breaks your strategy down into the following three key sections:

1. **Fan experience and engagement**: We've touched on this quite a lot in the last few chapters, but we're going to dive a bit deeper into how this translates into your ticketing strategy. We'll be looking at communicating with fans and soliciting feedback as well as some examples of what good looks like at some of the clubs that we work with at Kaizen.

2. **Revenue optimisation**: As much as we want people to have a great time when they visit or interact with our club, we also need to be mindful of how revenue is generated. The obvious areas of making tickets affordable, sustainable pricing, non-match-day revenue and using other club assets will all be covered here.

3. **Operational excellence**: Having a well-oiled machine that makes your operation look effortless is hard. How can you get your operation running with ruthless efficiency while keeping a personal and tailored feel for the supporters? Ticketing is crucial here and we also need to look at it through the lens of community integration, how you use data and sustainability.

The final takeaway as we prepare to build your ticketing strategy out is to remember that it is OK for it to evolve. Don't look at this as the process of writing a long document that is read once, put in a drawer and never referenced again. In fact, it should be quite the opposite.

Life at a football club can change rapidly. A promotion or relegation can have a big influence on the budget available. A player signing or sale can influence the level of interest as can a change in ownership. If something significant happens, the strategy should be flexible enough to adapt to the new circumstances – that is totally fine.

Getting into the habit of having check-ins with senior staff around the club to make sure that the strategy is still applicable is a good thing. A short review every three months will mean you're generally making small tweaks to the plan rather than huge changes once a year.

I have shared a strategy document template with you in the additional resources. This is designed to get you started if you're not sure where to begin. Feel free to add or remove areas that you feel are more applicable to your club or situation. As we go through the next few chapters, we can get you thinking about what is most important for you at your club. You'll rely less on the template and take your strategy off in the direction that works best for where you are currently and where you want to go next.

ALL TICKET

> **TAKEAWAY TASK: Don't set and forget**
>
> Take a look at the strategy document template in the resources section (www.kaizenticketing.com/resources) and familiarise yourself with the different areas of the document. Don't fill it out yet but keep these areas in mind as you progress through the upcoming chapters.

EIGHT
Fan Experience And Engagement

Improving the fan experience has been a hot topic at many football clubs lately. Looking at the way the club engages with supporters and improving or modernising that has been a priority for some. In this chapter, we're going to dive into some of the things that clubs are doing to improve these areas. You may already be doing some yourself, but I'm sure you'll also pick up a few new ideas or get some inspiration from the examples I'm going to share with you.

The big shift we are seeing with most clubs now is towards an increased openness to fans. Historically, clubs have been a pretty closed shop. A single investor buys a football club, and the club gets run with a top-down, 'my way or the highway' type of approach. The supporters are interested in what is happening but aren't told much, or they find out when the change has been made. Over time, their patience wears thin. They feel like they're being taken for granted and are generally underappreciated. Some vote with their feet and attendances decrease; some stick with it begrudgingly but are quick to voice their discontent from the stands. You can see how this isn't a sustainable approach for any club, but it's happened over and over through the years.

Thankfully, we've moved away from this and times are changing for the better. Most clubs these days are far more progressive and open. It is pleasing to see details emerge almost every week of clubs launching new supporter feedback groups, creating a place on the board for a fan representative and engaging in dialogue about key decisions before any action is taken, not to mention a host of clever initiatives to make younger or underrepresented groups feel welcome and part of the club.

It starts with everyone else

If this is the first time you've given any serious thought to your strategy around fan engagement, I urge you to avoid the most common mistake. Don't make it about the club, make it about the fans and your commercial partners. If you start here, you can't help but create a strategy that will be inclusive, engaging and original.

What do I mean about not making it about the club? Well, it would be fair to ask 'What do we want out of this?' as you're coming up with ideas. It's not a bad question, but it will guide all of your thinking or solutions to be just about the club's interests. In some cases, this will align with the wants and needs of your supporters; in other cases, not so much.

Some better questions might be:

- How can we use the assets we have to serve the local community?

- How can we use our brand to shine a light on important social issues?

- How can we make sure that our supporters know they are appreciated by us?

- What will make the club an attractive destination for all on match days or non-match days?

- Where are the next generation of supporters coming from?

- What qualities will make us a desirable commercial partner in a competitive market?

As you start to unpack these questions, you'll uncover areas that you want to improve as a club or share things that you wish you had had the time to introduce already. Thinking through your answers to these questions will help you introduce things that have a positive impact on groups associated with the club. Give it a try and let me know how you get on.

Technology is an enabler, not the star of the show

I spoke about this at length in Chapter Four, so I'm sure this is at the forefront of your mind as you begin to think about the role technology plays in your strategy. When it comes to improving the experience of the people who interact with the club, technology will be a key component. You're either going to be replacing something to drive an improvement or introducing something new. When it comes to software, I'm a product person. I cut my teeth learning how to build digital products for sports tournaments. One of the earliest and most useful things I learned about good products was that the best ones just operate in the background, without you even having to think about using them.

That is an idea we've carried into building our platform at Kaizen. The biggest compliment is when someone tells us that something looks 'clean' or 'intuitive'. There are a lot of complicated things happening behind the scenes, but we'll try to keep that out of the view of the person using the platform. Think of your technology selection in the same way. If you have to tell people how to use a particular piece of technology more than once, if you have to keep reminding them that it exists, and if people are questioning what it's there for in the

FAN EXPERIENCE AND ENGAGEMENT

first place, then it's likely either not the right choice or not working so well.

It shouldn't feel like you or your supporters are fighting with new technology or new processes. It's there to support. You already know that just because you can doesn't mean you should. Sometimes when you bring in something new, it'll get worse before it gets better, so I'm not saying the right product will bring instant results. Please make sure that you do your due diligence and, especially when it comes to introducing new systems, your technical due diligence. Make the wrong choice now and you could be stuck with something that isn't fit for purpose for a lot longer than you want.

CASE STUDY: Is it any easier at supporter-owned clubs?

Exeter City are a Kaizen client and at the time of writing, they are the highest-ranked supporter-owned club in England, playing in EFL League One.

The club has an incredibly forward-thinking approach when it comes to engaging with supporters and in particular the youngsters who represent their fans for future generations. We have worked closely with the club to help them automate many ticketing benefits associated with their Supporters' Trust membership.

The Supporters' Trust has played a huge role in the recent history of the club. After purchasing a majority shareholding of the club in 2003, it has been pivotal in preserving the club's legacy, from clearing the club's debts in tougher financial times to overseeing stand developments and supporting the local community through the City for All ticket scheme. The club's ticketing manager, Fred Burford, told us a bit more about the importance of the Trust in the club's ticketing decisions and strategy.

'Trust members will always get ticket priority for every league or cup match we play – home and away. It's our way of acknowledging what the Trust has done for the club over the years and I can't see that ever changing.

'The Trust is accessible to anyone. It only costs £2 per month to be part of and has been that way since 2004. We also have our Junior Grecian membership for our younger fans. That converts to a Trust membership when they turn sixteen. We do a lot for the Junior Grecians to keep them engaged with the club. There is a chance to train with the team every year and we set aside fifty free tickets per home league match for a Junior Grecian to attend with an adult.'

Fred also makes the point that the Trust membership means that having a say in how the club is run is open to anyone.

'Trust members are voted onto the board and can serve for a three-year period. They can remain on the board for a maximum of nine consecutive years. The great thing about this is that if there are supporters who feel they can contribute to improving the club, there is nothing to stop them standing for board status. Their fellow trustees will vote for them if they believe they are the right person for the job.'

You might feel a bit overwhelmed with all of the possible choices when it comes to creating this part of your ticketing strategy. Let's go through a few areas that I think will help you to decide what is important for your situation.

Fan surveys

Lots of clubs start the process off with a survey that is shared across all of their social channels, posted on the club website and emailed out to the supporter database if one exists. If you're looking for some ideas or just confirmation on the areas that you think are important for fans, then a survey can serve you well.

My biggest advice is to make sure you're targeting the right people. On more than one occasion, I've spoken with clubs that have run surveys and then implemented many of the suggestions that have been made by fans. They are then left disappointed when the fans don't make use of some of the new things they've introduced, based on that survey feedback.

Sometimes it's just unfortunate timing. In other cases, the fans who complete the survey aren't representative of the ones who actually go to games. That is why it is important to make sure that you're getting your survey in front of the right people. As tempting as it may be to blast everyone across as many channels as possible, you may not be getting answers from the people that you really need to speak to.

As a starting point, be clear about what you want to learn. Are you asking people's opinion about the match day experience, stadium facilities or pricing, for example? If you are, then I'd be inclined to be more targeted with an initial survey. Can you identify people who have been to a match in the last twelve to eighteen months, for example, or people who have only been once and not returned? These people are more likely to give you good feedback, relevant to the area you want to learn most about. Quality answers over quantity.

Maybe you're thinking about engaging better with international fans or supporters who aren't local. In that case, a different set of people will have the answers you need to help you improve things. Start off with the question 'What do I want to learn most about?'

If you're stumped for ideas, here are some to get you thinking.

Stadium experience

- Buying tickets
- Transport to and from matches

- Getting into the stadium on time
- Wayfinding and signage – eg getting to seats or finding toilets
- Atmosphere and safety
- Catering
- Pre-match, half-time and post-match entertainment
- Repeat visits
- Comfort and cleanliness of facilities

Community/new supporters

- Club presence in the local area
- Memberships
- Family areas or incentives to buy
- How fans were introduced to the club
- Suggestions for how the club could do more with schools, youth groups, local businesses, charities etc

Away matches

- Reasons people do/don't attend away games
- Satisfaction with information and rules on buying away tickets

- Club-organised travel

Communication

- Rating the club's communication channels and approach
- Responsiveness to supporter feedback or queries
- Satisfaction with club website/app
- Preferred channels and any untapped opportunities

Club identity

- Sense of the club's traditions, history and values
- Perspectives on diversity and inclusion around the club
- Views on quality and affordability of club merchandise

Reciprocity is key

Getting new people to visit the club for the first time may be a bit challenging, but it is certainly achievable. The real skill is in getting them to come back again and again.

Depending on who you speak to, you might hear opposing views on whether the performance on the pitch is directly responsible for increases or decreases

FAN EXPERIENCE AND ENGAGEMENT

in attendance. Some people will base team performance on their decision to turn up or stay away, but I'm firmly in the camp that it generally doesn't matter. If your stadium is a place that fans enjoy coming to, if it has a great atmosphere and supporters feel valued when they are there, the majority of fans will come and support through thick and thin. The key is giving people a big enough reason to want to come back again – which is exactly what you should be striving for.

I bet you have experienced an example of reciprocity more than once this week, without even realising it. It's the key to unlocking solutions to the ongoing challenge of getting one-off supporters to become regular attendees. Think about how many times in the last month you have been tempted to give something a try or move from being interested to making a commitment as a result of one of the following:

- A free trial or sample
- A complimentary offer, like buy one get one free
- Something being highly personalised to you or your needs
- Access to a special offer or product – limited to a privileged few
- Useful information or knowledge shared with you at no cost
- Feeling loyal to a brand because of the way they've made you feel as their customer

Reciprocity is so frequent in our daily lives that many of us don't even notice when it's happening. It is an old but gold tactic that has been used by many top brands and businesses for decades. When you've finished that slap-up meal in your favourite restaurant and it's time to pay the bill, why do you think the bill arrives with a few mints, sweets or a little gift for the table?

There are various studies and stats on this. When one mint is delivered with the bill, a tip is expected to increase around 3%. Two mints get you up to 14%. It has even been claimed that when the waiter leaves one mint, walks away and then turns around and gives a second, the tips go up by 23%.[5] It's not just giving the gift – it's the way you give it that has an impact too.

Let's bring this back to your club. If you're internally resisting the suggestion as it involves 'free' and you're worried about 'the cost' of giving things away, don't fear – we are going to be clever about how to do it. It isn't always as black and white as giving away free tickets. For some clubs, that will be an appropriate tactic; others will find that it's not effective or not feasible if they're selling out most weeks.

I challenge you to think about what else you can use at the club that might be considered a valuable gift for

---

5. DB Strohmetz et al, 'Sweetening the till: The use of candy to increase restaurant tipping', *Journal of Applied Social Psychology*, 32/2 (31 July 2006), https://onlinelibrary.wiley.com/doi/10.1111/j.1559-1816.2002.tb00216.x

FAN EXPERIENCE AND ENGAGEMENT

your supporters. How can you use it to encourage a return visit? Here are some examples:

- Season ticket holders can bring a friend to a match for free

- A promo code to buy one get one free after your first visit to a match

- A voucher for a free drink or snack at the food kiosks inside the ground

- A discount or choice of free gift (from selected merchandise) in the club shop

- Upgrades to premium seating or hospitality if there is spare capacity

- Invitation to exclusive events such as behind-the-scenes tours for fans who have achieved a certain milestone – eg matches attended or money spent

- Photo opportunities, pitchside or training experiences with the playing staff and manager

- Exclusive access to digital content

- Recognition from the playing staff or manager with a signed card or merchandise

You can see where I'm going with this. You can mix and match some of these ideas and before long you'll be coming up with your own, which will be more specific to what you know your supporters will value the most. The key is to not devalue the paid version of the thing you're giving away, while making it high value enough for it to have a wow factor. Use the assets you have around the club; it shouldn't cost you an excessive amount to deliver. Even if you do need to spend a little, the return on that investment is huge if you've created a loyal supporter for life.

The final thing I will say on this is this tactic works best when the gift you give is both personalised to the recipient and unexpected – so don't be boring or generic. Use gifts to recognise achievements or behaviour and leave the supporters thinking, *Wow, this is why I love my club.*

Lucky number seven

As a child, deciding which football team you're going to support is a big decision – maybe a decision you don't realise the long-term consequences of at the time. In the UK, it is extremely tribal. You will often hear people say things like 'Well my dad was a [insert team] supporter, so I had to follow.' Or 'I grew up in [insert area], so I had to support them.' If you get found out as someone who isn't from the area or has no family links to the team you support, you might get labelled as a 'glory hunter' – assuming there is any glory associated with your team on the pitch.

In other parts of the world, things are different. I will never forget my inability to comprehend some of my North American colleagues openly telling us that they

FAN EXPERIENCE AND ENGAGEMENT

were switching to supporting another team because they were moving to that part of the country.

I do think that this behaviour is slowly becoming more accepted here in the UK, and this is to the benefit of any football club outside of the top tier that isn't sold out every week. Lifetime loyalty still exists and that is part of what makes football in the UK unique, but with that also comes the common belief – not always true – that it is nearly impossible to get a ticket for your favourite football club or, if you can, it is overpriced.

People want value for money. An affordable day out, a decent atmosphere and an acceptable standard of football to watch. It is now more common than ever to find fans of a top-tier team watching EFL or non-league football and adopting a second team because of all of the good things on offer at an attractive price. You also have a group of people known as 'ground hoppers', who travel the length and breadth of the country week after week, looking to experience matches at all levels. This is a massive opportunity for you.

It is widely believed that a child forms an affiliation with their club at around seven years of age. This is usually the time when kids in schools start to pretend to be their footballing heroes in the playground – they're old enough to care about which team they want to be associated with. The savvy club should be using this knowledge to make sure they have a steady stream of new supporters coming through the ranks.

A great example of a club doing exactly that is Brighton & Hove Albion. They've experienced huge growth in the last fifteen years. Significant investment in the club has seen them rise through the leagues and relocate to a new, modern stadium.

I want to take you back, however, to 2010, when their average crowd was in the region of 5,000–6,000 in a converted athletics stadium, Withdean, close to the city centre. While waiting for the move to their new, permanent home at the now widely known and established American Express Stadium – where they attract an average sold-out attendance of close to 32,000 – Brighton were concerned that they'd potentially lost a generation of fans and started the work to get young supporters interested in the club. They launched an initiative that gave any child registered with the club as a member a free shirt on their seventh birthday. It went down extremely well, and the club saw more and more locals signing up. You just have to take a look at some of their fans' forums online to see proud parents talk about the loyalty that was created and how those appreciative seven-year-olds are still going to watch matches with them many years later.[6]

---

6. tshego, '"Lessons can be learnt abroad," says Brighton FC CEO at #sibc', Sport Industry Group (21 February 2017), www.sportindustry .biz/news-categories/news/lessons-can-be-learnt-abroad-says -brighton-fc-ceo-sibc, accessed 2 May 2025

CASE STUDY: Creating lifetime supporters

I was lucky enough to grab some time with Paul Barber, the chief executive and deputy chair at Brighton & Hove Albion. Paul is someone I worked with at both The FA and Tottenham Hotspur in years gone by. He is one of the most respected leaders in English football. He shared some great insight around how this initiative took off and evolved as the club grew.

'The club originally did some research on this around twenty years ago,' said Paul. 'Ray Bloom, who is a director here, was the person that led it. Ray has served on the board of Brighton and lower-level Worthing and has really seen the game at all levels over numerous decades. He is one of the longest-serving directors in football. He was keen to make sure the club didn't become complacent in attracting younger fans.

'Ray confirmed two key things in his research. Children were influenced by a family member, usually their father, in picking the team they would support. He also found that they typically made that decision around the age of seven years old.

'The club acted on this information and encouraged parents to register their children with the club. On their seventh birthday, the club sent a home shirt to every registered child. The goal was to get a Brighton shirt to every child in the area.'

This was a great strategy for the club, as they worked on growing their younger supporter base. I

ALL TICKET

was keen to find out how they managed to keep up with demand as the club continued to rise through the leagues.

Paul went on to add, 'It's a tradition we've kept going up to the present day. We've had to put a few more rules in place as the club has grown, so it is now part of a junior membership. The main rule we have now is that the junior must be registered for the season prior to their seventh birthday to be eligible for their free shirt.

'"Make it special" is one of our club values. In keeping with that, we sometimes send a player or club official out to deliver shirts personally to the juniors, which always goes down well.'

Paul was also clear on the positive commercial impact the initiative has on the club. He added, 'As well as being popular with juniors, it's great for the club. We have youngsters proudly wearing their kits around town. When I first moved here, I would drive past kids playing football on my local playing fields at the weekend and you would see some Brighton kits but also a lot of the Manchester teams, Arsenal, Tottenham, Chelsea etc. These days, most of the children on those playing fields are wearing Brighton colours.

'We think around 50% of the junior members go on to be lifetime fans. The initiative drives sales of future kits as the juniors want to keep up to date as new kits are released and we're now seeing those early junior members having kids of their own and, of course, continuing the tradition by signing their children up for a junior membership.

'It makes commercial sense. We use our membership data to make sure we have enough kits on order for the next round of birthdays. We're creating lifelong supporters for the cost of a home shirt. It's a tradition that we are extremely proud of and one we will do everything to continue for years to come.'

Partnerships with schools and youth teams

In keeping with the theme of the next generation of fans, the obvious place to start is local schools. Some clubs do the traditional fifteen-minute visit during an assembly, dump 100 free tickets in the headteacher's office and then disappear for six months. They will then say 'We've tried that, but it doesn't really work for us.'

The most effective way I've seen school visits done was by one of the early clubs that we worked with back in 2017, Billericay Town. The club had just been bought by a local businessperson, who happened to be a master marketer who knew how to get the local and national spotlight on his club.

The club would send a player and someone else from the club into a school. They would do a session with the children about the importance of healthy eating and exercise. The player would talk about the sacrifices that need to be made to become a professional footballer and the importance of education and having a career path after football. The sessions were done in smaller groups than the usual, school-wide assembly – closer to normal class sizes. At the end of the session, the children would all be invited by the player to come to the match on Saturday with a parent or guardian.

Remember what I said earlier: reciprocity works best when the gift you give is personalised to the recipient and when it is unexpected. Imagine being a seven-year-old who has just had a real footballer come and spend time in your class at school and invite you to come and watch them play at the match on Saturday. You would be begging your parents to take you.

Multiple sessions were done most weeks, and we helped the club to make the process digital so they could collect the parents' data for future marketing as well as track usage of the free tickets and return visits to see how well it was working over the season.

Where the club got this so right was the match day experience. It's one thing getting people there, but they have to have a good time. He invested a lot in improving the ground facilities. The bar area was extended and more food and drink outlets were added around the ground. The famous penny sweet shop in the clubhouse did great business with the influx of schoolkids now attending, and the players were always visible after matches, chatting with the supporters and signing autographs for the kids.

The main thing I want you to take from this is that you need to do more than just give away free tickets to schools. Give the children a reason to feel more connected to the club. You may not be able to afford the time for players to visit every week, which is understandable. There are other things you can do that generate just as much excitement and engagement from schoolchildren. For example, you could invite a class or youth team to be mascots for the day, offer children from a nearby school the opportunity to be ball retrievers at a match, or create a behind-the-scenes tour for schoolkids on a non-match day.

Experiences live long in the memories of children and one of these at the right time could be the thing that gets a young person involved with the club for the first time. If they have a great first time, chances are they will want to come back again and again.

First impressions count

Something else that should be in your thinking is first-time visitors. This is a big part of the criteria for the EFL Family Excellence Scheme I mentioned in the previous chapter. You can create a good or bad experience before someone has even visited your ground on match day.

Something that is becoming increasingly popular with many clubs is a digital first-time visitor guide. There are many ways to format one and a lot will depend on what information is crucial for someone visiting your stadium. I have linked to some good examples in the additional resources for you, if you're looking for a bit of inspiration.

This guide should be easy for people to find so those who need it know about it. The clubs that we work with tackle this in different ways. Again, there's no right or wrong approach – do what works best for your situation. To help promote the guide, you could include a link to it whenever someone purchases tickets, share it on your social media channels, send a specific email including the guide to first-time visitors two to three days before a match, and have it as a prominent feature on the club website.

If you do as much as you can to remove the stress of what to expect by outlining in advance where to find things, timings, costs and good local knowledge, your first-time fans will become regular attendees before you know it.

Get the foundation right

Having a solid fan experience should be the foundation of the strategy that you're putting together. You can have the most innovative systems and clever promotions but if visiting your stadium is horrible, you're just papering over the cracks, unfortunately.

FAN EXPERIENCE AND ENGAGEMENT

Your supporters want to feel valued. This will be reflected not just in how much they pay to watch their team but also in how much you invest in the facilities you provide when they come to visit. They want to feel safe. The quality of the stewards is important. Do they look professional and like they want to be there?

Most importantly, supporters want to be heard and understood. As I've said a few times throughout the book, meet them where they are. Once you've done that, you can then start to bring them along with you. Don't force new technology on them if they're not ready. Take the time to introduce things slowly. Communicate and help them to understand why change is necessary and how it will benefit them and the club they care about for years to come.

Remember that it should be about everyone else – your supporters, commercial partners and community. If you get that bit right, you can't help but create a winning strategy.

NINE
Revenue Optimisation

The next part of your strategy is all about revenue. This is something that I've become fascinated with as I've helped clubs to find ways of increasing it. There are some patterns that you'll see over and over, but the truly consistent theme is you'll always learn something new in the process of generating new revenue streams. I'm going to share many of my learnings with you in this chapter and give you some food for thought in the process.

The key question in ticketing, which has come up a few times in this book, is 'Are you trying to get more people in the ground or get the people who are already there to spend more money?' Revenue is of interest when your focus is on the latter.

ALL TICKET

It will come as no surprise when I say that to get your supporters to increase their spending, you need to make sure you're treating them well. If you've found any glaring flaws or issues with your approach to fan engagement, make sure you've addressed anything major first.

My advice here is similar to my opening advice in the previous chapter: when you set out making the revenue strategy focussed solely around your interests, it doesn't tend to work. The less transactional you are, and more values-driven you become, the more positive the impact on your revenue will be. That isn't to say I'm advocating a reckless 'it will work itself out' approach. We're trying to find a delicate balance where your supporters feel like they are getting good value for money and you feel the things you are offering them are viable.

The first and most obvious place to begin is ticket pricing. It's not an exact science and the approach that works for you will be dependent on your objective as a club. The club CEO and finance director should be able to give you a clear direction on this. Some clubs prioritise season ticket sales, as they like the perceived security of lump sums of cash coming in over the summer and ahead of the season starting. I know of other clubs that choose not to push season ticket sales too much, as they value the higher price that supporters will pay for individual match tickets. Some clubs like the cash in the bank over the summer. Others are quite happy to receive it throughout the season through subscriptions or instalments.

None of these are wrong, but knowing which one is right for you requires you to have an understanding of your supporters' buying patterns. You could argue that relying on match ticket sales is a riskier strategy and, in some cases, I would tend to agree. You only need a few postponed matches due to bad weather or your opposition being involved in a cup run and it impacts your cash flow. As a general rule, a weekend match rearranged for a weekday will draw a smaller crowd, so there's potential lost revenue there too.

On the flip side, if you're not impacted by adverse weather or cup runs and you have a healthy number of supporters buying match tickets in advance, then the additional money made per ticket (compared to the pro rata price paid by a season ticket) may well be worth the risk.

Draw on metrics

What metrics are going to help you to know which one is better for you? Ideally, you'll have access to at least a couple of seasons' worth of purchase data. Three patterns I would urge you to look for would be (these are generic enough to help pretty much any club):

ALL TICKET

1. **Percentage of advance sales versus percentage of match day sales.** Why? This tells you if there's work to do to get advance sales in the bank nice and early. If you have a traditionally late-buying crowd or a particularly high percentage of ticket sales on match days, it's going to be risky to rely on that revenue. People aren't committing early, so all it takes is a bit of rain or a better offer and they will miss the odd game or two, which adds up over the season.

2. **Season ticket attendance rates.** Why? If you're giving a bit too much value away with your season ticket pricing (or, some may say, undercharging), then this is where you'll see the first clue that this is the case. This is interesting because regardless of price changes, we've seen a correlation between more football being shown on TV and season ticket usage reducing over the last couple of seasons. Normally, the quick fix on this one lies with junior season tickets. Make them too cheap and people snap them up just in case they want to bring the kids, but in most cases they go unused. Whether to put the price up is a real tough dilemma, especially if you're a family-orientated club or you want to encourage more children at matches.

3. **Number of sold-out matches.** Why? Put simply, do you have spare capacity to play with? If seats are at a premium, you'll have an understandable reason to charge accordingly. You can apply this principle to specific parts of your ground too. If

there are certain areas that are always first to sell or are highly sought after, that might be your signal to review your pricing or introduce a resale scheme if supporters can't make certain matches.

There is plenty to think about, and the drivers for everyone reading this book will all be different. That's why I love the challenge. It's highly personalised and knowing your supporters is key to getting it right. Use these patterns as your starting point and then layer in additional context relevant to your situation. If you're struggling for a bit of inspiration or with knowing where to get started, here are some common tactics we've used to help clubs increase revenues. Remember, though, that this isn't a copy and paste exercise – look at these in the context of your club.

- Increasing prices the closer to match day people buy
- Upselling merchandise or hospitality when people buy online
- Gift vouchers and flexi tickets – the amount that goes unused is free money
- Combining ticket sales with other non-ticket items online for increased basket value
- Segmented emails, targeting likely purchasers
- Making sponsorship visible where people are buying tickets – you'll get some impulse purchases

Become a destination

Another area that should absolutely be part of your strategy is non-match-day revenue. It's taken clubs a little while to really start using the asset that is their stadium on days when no football is being played.

Your ground doesn't have to be in the best of conditions. You may not have the luxury of a modern stadium, but I bet you still have at least one, if not more, of the following facilities: outdoor space (eg car parking areas), a bar or clubhouse, an outdoor fan zone, a function room, retail space, office space, gym facilities. The list goes on, but what I'm advocating is using the space and areas you have. You will be able to create new and alternative ways of generating revenue on non-match days. Many clubs around the country are doing this already – here are some examples that might inspire you:

- Business networking groups in club lounges (some even host them on the evening of a match and throw in a free match ticket) – a great way of discovering new potential partners too

- Concerts or boxing events on the pitch in the off-season

- Hiring lounges for corporate events, coffee mornings or meetups

- Using hospitality bars and lounges for birthday parties, wakes and anything else in between

REVENUE OPTIMISATION

- All-day music festivals in the outdoor fan zones in the summer

- Screenings of international tournaments (mainly England matches) in their usual fan zone or clubhouse

- Hiring parts of a large car park for construction companies to host scaffolding-training workshops

- Converting a disused part of a stand and renting it out as serviced office space

- Converting hospitality boxes to hotel rooms and offering accommodation on non-match days

- Hiring adjacent pitches or training areas to local teams or youth competitions

While generating additional revenue is the primary benefit when you look to use your ground in this way, don't overlook the potential for valuable data capture here too. When you're hosting events that will bring a new audience to your stadium, you have a great opportunity to get them interested in the club and your primary business. Offering a quick stadium tour or even just a short welcome speech from a club official can be enough to get an unlikely new supporter interested. These new visitors are your potential season ticket holders, club sponsors or suppliers of the future, so don't miss a golden opportunity.

Club memberships

Club memberships can be an amazing opportunity to generate additional revenue, but there are a few caveats that come with them. The biggest mistake I see clubs make when launching new memberships is a lack of value in what the supporter receives for the membership fee. The days of supporters paying for a club membership, getting a pin badge and a thank you letter are long gone – people want more for their hard-earned money these days and quite right too.

The other common mistake is introducing too many variations of membership. It is what many of the 'big' clubs do, but for good reason. They have the enviable problem of demand and supply: hundreds of thousands, if not millions, of people around the world who want to be affiliated with the club in some way. In this scenario, it makes sense to offer a few different types of membership for people to choose from. In most cases, if you're starting out with a new membership scheme, starting with a simple option is the way to go.

Let's address what good value looks like in a membership. The starting point is being clear on who the membership is for.

If your club has identified that it needs to do some work to appeal to the younger generations, then a child membership is a great tool to help fuel that growth. As

REVENUE OPTIMISATION

we saw in the Brighton example in the previous chapter, a timely birthday present is of huge value and helps to cement loyalty to the club for many years to come. Experiences go a long way with child memberships too. Exeter City's Junior Trust membership offers a limited number of young members a chance to train with the team. An experience like that is only going to strengthen a child's affiliation with their club and inspire them to want to play there one day.

Looking at adult memberships, the value in a ticketing context is usually going to be advance access or favourable pricing. Being conscious of where you are as a club will determine what is best for you. There is no point in launching a membership that guarantees advanced access to all league match tickets if you rarely sell out your league matches and it's usually possible to turn up and pay on the day. Packing your membership with lots of value will require you to look at what you already have access to at the club, as you did with fan engagement. You can also offer benefits in circumstantial cases to increase that perceived value.

About three years ago, I helped one of our clubs introduce a new membership structure to their fans. At the time, their average attendance was just under 1,000 people per match in a stadium that held over 5,000 – so plenty of room to grow into. They used membership as a revenue generator. They didn't have a supply and demand problem, so they used the membership as a way to add more value for people that were already attending matches. This is what they offered:

- A slightly reduced ticket price for each member if they bought in advance and online
- A priority booking period for all cup matches
- A discount on selected drinks at the club bar on match days and non-match days
- A discount if you booked the club facilities for a function
- Access to a one-off group Zoom call with other members and the first-team manager
- A digital version of the match programme emailed for every home league match
- Match highlights emailed to members as soon as they were released
- A club shirt signed by the first-team squad
- Entry into two prize draws to experience being a club official for the day at a home or away match

As a club, they were making use of existing assets and infrastructure. A little bit of financial modelling was needed to work out what they could afford to discount on a match ticket, bearing in mind that every member wouldn't be attending every match. The same went for the bar discount, and while a discount on function room hire was generous, it was agreed that

REVENUE OPTIMISATION

any bookings from members would be additional, unbudgeted revenue – so essentially a bonus.

Priority booking for cup matches cost the club nothing and induced a sense of FOMO (fear of missing out). If the club do get to The FA Cup third round and draw Manchester City at home, every fan will want to be able to beat the rush and uncertainty of a general sale or a restricted sale where they don't meet the criteria.

They made use of digital assets and processes that they were already having to create. Emailing a digital programme costs nothing, and the same goes for the match highlights – both of which they had to produce anyway. The manager was willing to give up sixty minutes of his time, as he would have been used to doing from time to time as part of the club's fan engagement initiatives, and signed merchandise is something every club makes use of in various ways.

The interesting addition was the Club Official Experience, which would have been something the club could easily accommodate but was a valuable prize for any supporter who wanted to get a chance to feel what it's like to be an official for the day, sitting with club directors or travelling on the team coach. Minimal inconvenience for the club, but a once in a lifetime experience for a lucky fan.

You are an international business

When I make this observation to a club, sometimes they scoff and suggest there's no way anyone outside of their town or city would be interested in them, never mind people outside of the country. You might have the same belief, but I want to challenge you to think bigger. We first put this to the test in the early years of building the Kaizen platform. When we made it possible for clubs to sell merchandise and tickets together, we were in for quite a surprise.

The first club to use the new feature was King's Lynn Town. At the time, they were attracting gates of about 600 and playing at the seventh tier of the football pyramid in England. Their first sale was a home shirt to a supporter in Iceland. Sales to fans in Canada, Italy and Australia soon followed and we all realised there was a much bigger market out there.

We saw the same patterns with other clubs playing at a similar level and, of course, you will remember the story of Margate making themselves known to an international audience in Chapter Five.

I did a little bit of digging around the new-found international supporters of these clubs and the pattern was consistent. They were mainly fans who had connections with the local area, who had at some point moved away for work or family reasons. They wanted to stay in touch with the club in some way. It further strengthened the point – every club should be thinking internationally. People move away from the area but still want to be involved or show their support. For some it will be buying merchandise, for others that could be a membership.

Some savvy clubs have started to launch international memberships, specifically for this group of supporters. Just like in the example above, you can pack your international membership with tons of value, using digital and virtual assets that you already have. One club that we helped with setting this up went a step further and offered any international member up to two free home league match tickets as part of the membership for if they happened to be in England and wanted to come to a match. It was an amazing gesture, which was hardly taken up as most of the members weren't planning to travel over for a match; however, the perception of the free tickets made it a high-value offer.

Think low-cost and think creatively

An alternative approach you can take with membership is to collate lots of special offers with other partners. I know of a non-league club who agreed special offers and discounted rates with most of the local businesses in their town centre high street: things ranging from free eye tests and a discount on glasses at the opticians through to discounted drinks at a pub before Saturday matches. The result of their membership drive was

ALL TICKET

impressive. Lots of locals who hadn't been to the club before signed up to take advantage of the great offers available. New revenue for the football club, new and repeat customers shopping locally and a great range of offers for the members – everyone wins.

CASE STUDY: Building links with local schools

As well as your paying sponsors, you should also see local schools as your partners. A fantastic example of a club that we work with doing this well is Sutton United. The club created an affiliate scheme with some schools in the area. For every ticket purchased using a dedicated link, the club shares some of the revenue with the school in question.

This incentivises the school and parents to help market matches at the club as a way of raising funds, and the club can benefit from new fans attending and lots of potential repeat attendances in the future.

We have helped them to make the process easy to manage digitally. Trackable links and sales reporting that highlights which tickets were sold by who have helped them to make the process beneficial to the club and is not time-consuming to carry out.

Victoria Otto and Max Wilson have put in a lot of hard work to grow this incredible initiative. They were good enough to share their experiences in setting this up.

'We wanted to do more to involve the local community,' said Victoria. 'We saw Crystal Palace doing something similar and also learned that Aberdeen had been developing this kind of initiative over the last ten years or so.

'It seemed to be quite manual, so we looked for ways to use technology to make it feasible for us. The solution we have in place is a win for everyone. The club is being introduced to new fans, the school has a new way of raising funds, and we get to strengthen our ties with the community.'

Max added, 'Aberdeen were great in helping us get started and answered a lot of the how-to questions we had. Using technology has made it far easier to track the impact of each campaign and now that it is being promoted well, we have willing participants contacting us most weeks.

'Our next step will be to look at the data we've collected and see how we can encourage more of those young fans to come back more frequently.'

A quick word on virtual tickets

It wouldn't be right for me to write a whole chapter on ways of generating revenue and not mention virtual tickets. Back in the dark days of lockdowns and the global pandemic, a virtual ticket campaign was the thing that put our company on the map.

One of our clients, Marine AFC, had drawn Tottenham Hotspur in the third round of The FA Cup. At this

ALL TICKET

time, clubs were allowed no more than 600 supporters in their ground, due to social distancing guidelines that were in place. Just two weeks before the match, government rules changed again as England prepared to go into the third lockdown within twelve months. It was a blow for Marine as the little ticket revenue they could have made was taken away, and, to add insult to injury, a key match sponsor pulled out as there were no longer going to be people inside the ground to see the adverts that they would have on display as a sponsor.

Being the resourceful club that they are, Marine devised a plan to sell virtual tickets instead. It was, essentially, a donation; the original plan was to replace the lost ticket sales income by limiting sales to 600. We helped them set it up online and put it on sale and the 600 virtual tickets sold out in the first hour. Demand was high, so we kept going – the next target being 3,000, which was roughly the capacity of their ground. It wasn't long before they all went and demand was still high, so we kept going. Six thousand was the next target – that would beat the highest ever attendance to watch a match at Marine…Smashed that and still going strong. At this point everyone agreed that we should just keep going.

The story of this small club from Liverpool caught up in the magic of The FA Cup, the bad-luck story of the withdrawn sponsorship, and the misfortune of having no fans present to watch the biggest match in

REVENUE OPTIMISATION

the club's history had captured the hearts of the football community all over the world.

The campaign picked up pace and went viral. On the day of the match, we had already sold 16,000 virtual tickets. Then things ramped up as TV coverage started and presenters and pundits like Gary Lineker, Alan Shearer and Ian Wright all shared their support on their social media channels, urging even more fans to get involved. We finished the campaign with just over 33,000 virtual tickets sold – a massive 17,000 of those sold in a single day. I was so pleased for them when the attendance announced on the BBC's *Match of the Day* was 32,202.

It was a scary, yet thrilling, experience, and it became a great case study for us to share with other clubs, to prove that we had built software that could cope with huge demand.

A few clubs have tried to emulate Marine's success with virtual tickets since then, but no one has come close to those kinds of numbers. We have still helped clubs to generate significant revenues using this tactic, though, and some have even gone on to do virtual season tickets quite successfully. The conditions must be right to make it work, so if you're thinking of doing something similar, here's a little checklist that will help you:

1. **What is the story behind the need to do it?** Marine had the sponsor pull out and no

fans being allowed in as their reason. People immediately felt for them and were compelled to help. The answer to this question will make or break the success of the campaign.

2. **What is the target?** The momentum for the campaign was created in those first couple of days when there were targets announced publicly. First it was to replace the lost revenue from 600 tickets, then it evolved into breaking attendance records.

3. **What's in it for everyone?** While it was technically 'just a donation', the club offered to create a prize draw as a way of saying thank you. Signed merchandise and even the chance to manage the team for a game were all prizes on offer.

Have good answers to those three questions and I'm sure you'll nail it.

Do the best with what you have

When it comes to optimising revenue, make sure you're making the best use of what you already have. As a club, you have so many assets to tap into: everything from the playing staff, the club brand and reputation and the stadium facilities, to your partners and suppliers and, of course, matches every other week.

REVENUE OPTIMISATION

Using a little creativity, your unique knowledge of the club and your understanding of your supporters, you will be able to unlock new sources of revenue. The chances are there are some easy wins right under your nose – things you take for granted because they're just there every day. Willing partners and suppliers who are all too keen to get involved will help you get the wheels in motion.

I've added some additional ideas for generating revenue to the resource pack, so check that out if you want more ideas on ways to get started.

TEN
Operational Excellence

I want to take you with me into the future. We're not going too far – just eighteen months ahead of today, to see what things are like. It looks promising. You decided to finally take control of the ticketing strategy at your club after reading an inspiring book called *All Ticket*. It gave you plenty to think about and helped you put together a solid plan of action.

You started to implement some ideas from the book and things are already looking great. You identified ways of increasing attendances with your colleagues, set some targets, and you're seeing your numbers go up month by month. There's a sense of calm in the office now and everything you do seems less reactive. You had a chance to think about your season ticket renewal campaign before launching it this time, packed it with lots of additional value, and you've seen the highest renewal rate in club history, despite an average season on the pitch.

Here's the twist. When new fans come to the club for the first time, the first thing they see on the walk up to the stadium is a rickety old fence that is half collapsed on the ground. As they walk across the car park, they are greeted by two characters in the distance who look a bit menacing. One is wearing a stained, worn-out sweatshirt; the other is wearing a polo shirt and has a cigarette hanging out of his mouth. As fans get closer to them, one of them barks 'Tickets please.' You can see people relax a bit as they realise they work for the club. They look at people's tickets and direct them to the correct stand.

Some fans are early and decide to have a drink outside in the fan zone. The queue is long, but people join anyway. After ten minutes they finally get served a couple of pints of warmish, watered-down, semi-flat beer. It takes ages to pay by card because 'The Wi-Fi is a bit temperamental today.' They offer to pay cash but get told 'Correct money only please – we've run out of change.'

It gets closer to kick-off and everyone in the fan zone decides they'd better start getting inside. The queue for the turnstiles is massive and only getting worse as everyone is frantically trying to get to their seat for kick-off. The person scanning tickets keeps apologising

OPERATIONAL EXCELLENCE

for the slowness. They're telling everyone that it's their first day and they've not had any training, and the fans hear more excuses about the Wi-Fi again as the steward looks at what appears to be an ancient scanning device with a puzzled look on their face.

A group of fans get to their seats and find two of the four are broken. Not just a bit cracked, but half missing. They locate a steward, who shrugs his shoulders and shuffles around a bit, not knowing what to suggest. Eventually, a few thoughtful fans rearrange themselves and make space for the two seatless supporters to sit down and watch the match after missing the first ten minutes.

Half-time comes and it's more of the same. The queues at some of the concessions are not worth joining as they're too long. You can hear a few grumbles about the quality of the pies, so a few fans take a positive approach and joke about how they've dodged a bullet. The queue for the toilets isn't much shorter, and after some fans eventually make it inside, they're left wishing they had held on and gone somewhere else after the match.

The final whistle goes and there's a stampede to leave the stadium. It takes ages. More queues as thousands of people all try to get out through the same gates, all trying to get back to the pub or train station because there's nothing worth staying for.

This little glimpse into the future is what can happen if we don't pay any attention to the third and final part of our strategy: operational excellence.

I may have embellished parts of that stadium experience, but you can rest assured that I have seen all of them to some degree, visiting grounds around England. Maybe you can recognise some too?

I want to make sure that the importance of a great experience when someone visits your club is not lost on you. Creating a great experience goes way beyond an easy booking process or tickets saved in your mobile wallet. Both are important in their own right, but don't lose sight of the bigger picture.

Get rid of the barriers

Ultimately, we want to remove all of the reasons why someone would choose to not come to watch a match at your stadium. On those cold, wet December mornings when supporters have woken up with a bit of a hangover and realise they agreed to go to the match with their friends or family, sometimes knowing that it takes too long to get in or get served, the food is rubbish or expensive for what it is, or the seats are uncomfortable is enough of a reason to not go and to take the kids to the cinema or stay home and watch it on TV instead.

If you can remove the excuses that people have to not come, you're already winning. Some of these are easy

OPERATIONAL EXCELLENCE

wins, others may require some financial investment to fix, and others may not be completely in your control. In this chapter, we're going to look at what you can do and possibly what might be getting overlooked because it's almost too obvious.

I understand that you're probably not sitting on a huge pot of cash to build new toilets or rip out and replace all of your seats. If you know me, you'll know I'm a fan of old-fashioned stadiums. They have character, and when they're full, it creates an atmosphere that is hard to replicate in some of the more modern ones that have been built recently. Having an old stadium isn't an excuse for not having a slick operation, though. Let's take a look at the parts that are in our control and what we can do to create operational excellence at our venues.

Community integration and volunteering

Having local people involved in the match day operation can be valuable; I'd even go as far as to say essential. Someone who can pass on a seemingly simple bit of local knowledge to a visiting supporter is an important part of your team. Your club will be judged on the quality of those little bits of information, and no one wants to hear 'Sorry, I'm not sure' when they ask relatively straightforward questions like 'What's the fastest way to get back to the train station?' Don't underestimate the value of a bit of local knowledge – it goes a long way.

ALL TICKET

This won't be relevant to all clubs, but many rely on volunteers to make their operations work on a match day. For some clubs, this can be a bit of a double-edged sword. It's fantastic that some individuals will give up their time on evenings and weekends to help with the things that need to be done to put a match on. It's also good to be aware of people's motivations for it too. Many people want to give back, maybe feel like they're contributing to something if they're retired or out of full-time employment. Others are doing it for experience because they have aspirations to get a full-time, paid role working in the sports or events industry.

More often than not, volunteers also happen to be fans of the club, which can be a great thing. The benefit to them is being able to watch the match in exchange for doing some work. This is where things can get a little tricky. As you will know, in most operational roles the work doesn't stop when the match kicks off. Asking someone to keep working when they're doing it for free and are also a fan of the club can be an awkward conversation.

For that reason, some clubs' operations fall short. Volunteers rush to get things done so they can get in for kick-off or, even worse, abandon what they're doing because the match is about to start. I've seen it happen on a few occasions. Quite often the club will sympathise because it's unpaid work. I can understand that viewpoint. The fair compromise can be to work things out on rotation. Have one person stay after kick-off to

OPERATIONAL EXCELLENCE

make a few late sales in the club shop one week. The following match, they get to go in early and someone else takes 'the late shift'.

I do know of a couple of clubs that insisted on paid work only as soon as they could afford to do it. In those cases, the owners either had the means or the club started to generate the means to pay for their match day staff. It removed any ambiguity around roles, and if you had previously volunteered, you had a choice to continue working a full shift until half-time and be paid for it or attend matches as a fan again.

Training is essential

Volunteers or not, I'm a firm believer that anyone who is fan-facing should be trained in their role and shouldn't be dealing with supporters until they're at the required standard to perform that role.

Stewards are usually the first club representative someone will interact with on match days. These people are giving a first impression of your club. Start with simple things like looking the part – giving them a club tie or high-visibility coat, for example. It should be obvious looking at them that they represent the club. Similarly, turnstile staff should be adequately trained, especially if they're scanning tickets or taking payments on the gate. I've witnessed far too many occasions when someone has been thrown in for the first time with a two-minute briefing on how to work a card terminal and then expected to get on with it. It's admirable if that's all they need to get going, but in most cases they're not confident enough or equipped with enough knowledge to take payments quickly and keep the queues moving. The same can be said for scanning tickets. It's a simple job when the ticket is valid, but what should they do when it's not? What do they need to check for, who should they send people to etc? A person being able to pass on information confidently makes supporters feel like they're being dealt with by a professional.

CASE STUDY: Bringing it all together – a model transformation

EFL club Mansfield Town FC is a great example of the success that comes from putting many of the things that have been discussed in this book into practice. Kaizen started working with the club as a ticketing partner in the summer of 2022. There was a strong culture of 'pay on the day' among the supporters, largely caused by a challenging process if you wanted to buy tickets in advance online. The ticket office would sell in the region of 600 tickets face to face on the day of the match, which meant a lot of queuing and a stressful day for everyone.

Historically, season tickets had been processed manually by a small team in the ticket office. The application process consisted of submitting paper forms with a long wait time for anyone wanting to

OPERATIONAL EXCELLENCE

move seats. The software they used for monitoring entries into the stadium through the turnstiles was being discontinued, so there were a number of new things that needed to be introduced at the club over the summer.

We started off by offering season ticket renewals and new purchases online for the first time. The benefit was clear for all to see as they equalled the previous season's sales in the first week of the new sales campaign. Season tickets could be delivered as mobile tickets that were added to a supporter's mobile wallet, or they could pick a traditional season card if they preferred something physical to keep.

A bespoke integration with their automated turnstiles allowed us to create an entry dashboard so the safety team could monitor scan rates into the stadium. We worked with the club safety officer and their SAG to ensure they had all the information they needed to stay compliant with the safety guidelines.

The biggest impact of this work was in the subsequent two seasons as they continued to break their season ticket records every year. Matches started to sell out consistently around a week in advance and on the rare occasions there were tickets for sale in the week leading up to match day, it would be tens rather than hundreds. Their matches have been the definition of 'all ticket'. When it was possible, they encouraged visiting clubs to sell tickets digitally to their fans through their platform to reduce the time needed to print paper allocations, saving everyone time, stress and additional costs. The club introduced a loyalty programme to help manage the demand for away match tickets and they saw a 42% increase in the selection of digital season tickets as their older supporters started to become more comfortable with the technology.

Alex Sherriff is the operations director at the club and knows a thing or two about the topic of operational excellence. This is what she had to say about the transformation that the club has been through.

'The changes we've seen at Mansfield Town over the past couple of seasons have been remarkable. Moving from match day sales and manual season ticket processing to a fully digital, streamlined operation has changed the way we work. The introduction of online sales, mobile ticketing and automated entry monitoring has not only improved our efficiency but also made the match day experience better for our fans.

'We've gone from long queues and last-minute sales to selling out matches well in advance, and that's made a huge difference to both the club staff and the fans. Season ticket sales are the highest they've ever been in the club's history. The expertise and support we've had from Kaizen has been invaluable. Without them, we simply wouldn't have been able to make these changes as effectively or as quickly. The impact on our day-to-day ticketing and match day operations has been transformational, we're in a far stronger position off the pitch.'

OPERATIONAL EXCELLENCE

Use historic data to improve match days

If you are striving for operational excellence, one of the most important things you should know is the profile of your supporters. Do you have slightly older fans as the majority? Factoring that into your stadium access decisions and even your policy on match day sales or things like going cashless or not will be key.

If you have strong attendance numbers from a younger demographic, you can perhaps afford to be a little more bold in your offering or introduction of new technologies. Obviously, in most cases, your club will have fans of all ages attending, so the key is making sure you're not excluding anyone. The art is knowing when to push harder for change because it's better for the club and not a major inconvenience for the fans.

There are lots of hidden clues to things that can be improved in the data you've accumulated from previous matches. As you create a little bit more time and space for yourself by implementing some of the methods in this book, you'll have more time to look at historic data to see how you can optimise your match day operations.

What kinds of optimisations could you make? Well, here are a few examples of things that clubs we work with have been able to improve, just from looking for patterns from previous sales:

- **Using historic sales data to predict on-day attendance:** They started to see a consistent pattern in the number of sales made by the Wednesday before a Saturday match. They used that number to make a solid estimate of the likely attendance, which helped them to staff up additional catering units and order in enough food for unexpectedly busier matches.

- **Looking at historic entry data to reduce queue times at certain gates:** After seeing a trend of the majority of supporters entering through a particular entrance, the club increased staffing and added more external attractions and catering nearer to other gates to encourage a spread of supporters and reduce queue times getting into the stadium.

- **Using entry data to encourage earlier attendance** (an older but popular one): Clubs have rewarded fans for arriving earlier and entering the turnstiles with discounts or even sometimes free offers on food and drink at concessions inside the stadium. This has helped to reduce the number of supporters turning up five minutes before the match, which was causing heavy congestion at the turnstiles.

Operational excellence is everywhere

When you're building out the operational part of your strategy, a good thing to look for is areas that will

OPERATIONAL EXCELLENCE

reduce friction for both supporters and the club. There are some other areas that you could look at as you start to make these improvements around the ground.

The first, and one of the most common causes of grumbling at many of the grounds I've been to, is Wi-Fi. Good Wi-Fi at football grounds is rare. Sometimes there are constraints due to the location; sometimes it just hasn't been a priority. As clubs continue to turn to more and more digital solutions and have greater aspirations to engage with fans online, having fast, reliable Wi-Fi at the stadium gives you a great foundation to build on.

From a ticketing perspective, ticket entry scanning 'just happens' when the Wi-Fi is on point. It's possible to get by with offline modes as backup, but it should be exactly that – a backup plan. Having access to all that real-time scanning data with people being able to flow through the turnstiles rapidly should be the aspiration. Without it, you're limiting what you can do and causing unnecessary headaches for your staff and your fans.

One thing I will say if you're installing Wi-Fi is to make sure you're using a supplier who understands the potential numbers of people who will be congregated in certain areas both inside and outside the stadium. Strange things can happen when you have a large gathering of people all with mobile devices in their pockets. A supplier who doesn't have experience of football stadiums or large gatherings of people may overlook certain things as they install it, and you'll find that your Wi-Fi doesn't perform quite so well when it gets busy on a match day. As always, do your homework on your supplier, look for evidence and case studies of them working with other clubs like yours and ask lots of questions before you appoint them.

This can also have a knock-on effect on payment systems. Fast and reliable connectivity is essential for taking payments around the ground. That could be a chip and PIN machine at the turnstile, in the concourse or at the ticket office. If you have to wait for twenty seconds every time you process a payment, the queues will soon start to back up and you'll have some frustrated supporters to deal with. In the name of being operationally excellent, we want to make sure that we're getting people through the gates or served with food and drink as quickly and efficiently as we can. Not to mention the poor staff who have to deal with this week in, week out. You'll probably experience a high turnover of match day staff if they're being subjected to angry supporters each week.

I have seen some try to overcome the Wi-Fi problem with 4G SIM cards inside payment terminals, which isn't a great long-term solution. You'll also potentially have issues again when you have that large concentration of people with phones in their pockets and network speed starts slowing down. My advice is not to put a sticking plaster over the situation. Invest in the right infrastructure and then reap the rewards of happy staff and happy fans queuing up (briefly) to give you their money.

More recently, I've seen a wave of clubs focussing on sustainability around their match day operations, which is fantastic. Most notably, striving to reduce food waste or making sure that someone can make use of any unwanted food once the hospitality operations have finished. Some clubs have been making use of products like the Too Good To Go app (www.toogoodtogo.com), which is a platform that helps retailers to redistribute surplus food. You can create and sell 'surprise bags', which customers can buy through the app and come to collect from you.

Additionally, many clubs will distribute unused food to homeless shelters or people on the streets if they're subject to late postponements on a match day, when food has already been prepared for incoming hospitality guests and supporters.

Digital or paper, the choice is yours

It would be wrong if I didn't end the chapter by bringing it back to core ticketing. On the topic of operational excellence, the debate about eradicating paper tickets will often arise. It is an emotive topic for some fans. There is the argument that they love to have a physical souvenir for the day and something they can add to a collection and look back on over the years to come. The flip side is that printing paper tickets is time-consuming for staff and there are negative environmental impacts of both the production and distribution of paper tickets at scale.

ALL TICKET

I still think we're a little too early to start forcing digital tickets on everyone. I love them, and having come from the generation that still remembers 100% paper ticket venues, the improvements in efficiency and cost saving are phenomenal. At Kaizen we pushed some boundaries back in 2017 and ticketed the first ever 100% e-ticket match in the National League. Both home and away fans used digital tickets; there wasn't a single paper ticket in the stadium. Proving that it could be done left me feeling optimistic about the future. That was a little ahead of its time and is definitely less of a big story these days.

There are still supporters who will make a point of getting a paper ticket if one is available. Even putting up small barriers like making them collect or adding a small fee to the ticket doesn't deter them. I know of one club where a supporter buys online and then visits the ticket office every match and asks for his e-ticket to be reprinted to paper stock so he can keep it in his collection.

Supporters – they have their ways and quirky habits, but without them, there would be no club. We can come up with the most innovative products and slick new processes, but it will always be the supporters of the club who will decide if these are successful. Keep these people at the centre of everything you do and when you genuinely care about making things better for them, you can't help but win.

OPERATIONAL EXCELLENCE

It's been a while since I set you an end-of-chapter task, so here's the final one to keep you on track.

> **TAKEAWAY TASK: Be a role model**
>
> Sign your club up to a sustainable initiative if you're not doing something already. You could tackle food waste, recycling, carbon footprint reduction – there are plenty of choices. As a leading organisation in your community, set an inspiring example to follow.

Conclusion

A lot might have happened since you started reading this book. When you first picked it up, you were probably a bit stressed and overwhelmed. There's a fair chance that you were going through the motions week to week, reacting to the problems that were put in front of you and spending many of your days firefighting. Even worse, you may not have even realised it and were prepared to keep going with no end in sight.

You were looking at other clubs for some inspiration – trying out a modified version of their latest promotional campaign or offer. When it didn't work as well for you as they said it did for them, you were left wondering why, baffled as to why it seemed like everyone else was able to create consistent wins but your efforts kept falling short. This had been happening time and time again and you were slowly losing hope.

I hope the book has helped to give you a sense of where some of your blind spots may be. You should now feel like you've got some tools that will help you to make a plan to elevate the ticketing operation at your club – not only for the immediate future but also over the long term as well.

You have everything you need to create the ideal ticketing strategy. You also have a few tactics that can be used to give yourself the time and space to create it. That's important. If you can't get out of that defensive, reactive state, thinking strategically and long term is so much more difficult.

What you've learned

In the first part of the book, we unpacked our five C's of ticketing success – a method we have been using at Kaizen Ticketing to help clubs to take control of their ticketing operation. These are:

1. **Clarity**: We always start here to make sure everyone is clear on what they want the future to look like. Just getting through this process alone will help you to get better aligned with others around the club and limit the instances of people going off in conflicting directions.
2. **Captivate**: Once everyone agrees on what a successful future looks like, you can then start to

CONCLUSION

put together offers and campaigns that capture the attention of your supporters. This gets you out of the lottery of the 'let's just try stuff and see what works' mess that a lot of clubs find themselves in.

3. **Cutting-edge tech**: This might be the most daunting step for some and the most welcome change for others. The reality is that new and evolving technologies are available and will make our lives easier. The people who choose to master them will be the ones who win long term.

4. **Communication**: The success or failure of your efforts could be determined by this step. Having a thoughtful and timely message to share with the right people is what will set you apart from the organisations that play the numbers game and spam everyone with everything.

5. **Confidence**: To keep the success going, you're going to need to keep working on your own skills too, whether that's being on top of good customer service practices, brushing up on your technical skills or learning how you can make the most out of new features. These good habits will boost the confidence of you and your team.

As you implement some of these ideas in your daily operation, you'll start to create more time and space for yourself to think longer term. In the second part of the book, we looked at three key areas for you to consider as you build out your longer-term strategy.

Fan experience and engagement: It's been a buzzword for a while, but it's here to stay and the focus on it is greater season after season. The expectations of your supporters increase every year and the types of supporters you have to cater for are more varied than ever before. Online, offline, first-time, seasoned regular, young, old, local, international, diehard or casual – they all have expectations and it's your job to meet them.

Revenue optimisation: One of the many hats the modern ticketing manager needs to wear is that of the 'revenue generator'. These days it goes beyond clever pricing strategies or offers. While they're still important elements, you also need to be thinking about non-match-day revenue, using your stadium facilities to their full potential, recurring revenue and packing everything with so much value, supporters are lining up to give you their money.

Operational excellence: This is the cornerstone of every successful strategy. You can have the most clever, compelling and innovative approach on paper, but if you don't have a competent, confident, well-trained team to deliver it, the whole thing falls apart. It's possible to have high standards for paid staff or volunteers. The key is making sure everyone has the knowledge they need to deliver on the parts they are responsible for. Your job is to coordinate this with ruthless efficiency.

CONCLUSION

Going forward

I want to be crystal clear with you: this will not be easy or quick. This book is a result of me clarifying my thinking based on decades of trying and failing at all of these things. Sometimes things have gone well, really well in fact. Other times, I've been left disappointed at the outcome but have taken a big lesson away that I can use to improve my next attempt.

I have no doubt that it will be the same for you. There will be some trial and error and sometimes things won't go to plan. This is to be expected. The most important thing is that you don't give up when that happens to you. There is always something to learn from the situation, so take the learnings and make sure you apply them.

If you stick to the process, review the feedback and persevere, you will find yourself in a much better position over the long term. As I've said a few times throughout the book, consistency is so important. That is what makes this work.

If you're unsure where to start, you can take our scorecard quiz to get an objective view of your current situation. It only takes two minutes to complete and you'll receive a personalised report, giving you a score across the methods discussed in this book. Head over to https://scorecard.kaizenticketing.com to get started.

You'll also get access to our ticketing strategy canvas when you complete the scorecard. This is a nice tool that you can use with your colleagues. It will help you to keep focussed on the areas that matter most when you start to map out your strategy together.

I've created a resource pack to help you as you begin to implement the ideas that have been shared across the chapters. You can download it by visiting www.kaizenticketing.com/resources. It contains some tools and templates that will help you to get started quickly, generate your own ideas and, importantly, ask the right kind of questions as you start to navigate this in the context of your club.

I have also set up a community for people who have read the book and want to share ideas and learn from each other. Search Facebook for 'All Ticket Community' and you can join a private group. I am keen to build up a community of professionals who can help each other. I mentioned in an earlier chapter that this is something that I feel our industry has lacked for some time: a group with no agenda and no upsell, dedicated to our niche. I like to see things being done properly and if I can bring together a group of people who can help each other and bring the best out in each other, share good practice and see success in their ticketing operations, I will be delighted with that as the outcome.

Most importantly, I would love to keep the conversation going with you. If you think I can help you in

CONCLUSION

any way, please let me know. Whether it's thoughts on implementing the ideas in this book or working with our technology at Kaizen, I'd love to chat with you.

The purpose of me putting this book into the world is to try and encourage good practice. I want to share that knowledge with as many people as possible. This was something that wasn't readily available to me as I was finding my way in the ticketing industry, and much of what I learned was through trying things out and learning different skills in my own time. If I can save a few people a few years to get better outcomes, then we've both won.

Equally, if this book has helped you, I would love to hear about your wins too. Perhaps you've started to implement some of the ideas and seen positive changes. Tell me what they are and how things are going. I'm here to support you.

If you want to send me an email, send it to book@kaizenticketing.com. I will personally read all messages sent to that address – I'm looking forward to hearing from you.

There is a lot of work ahead for you, but as I said in the introduction, I'm excited for you. There is so much potential and opportunity in our industry at this time. You have access to a captive, global audience and you're alive during the biggest technology evolution the world has known. The stars have aligned and you are in the

ALL TICKET

perfect position to be someone who contributes to the growth of our industry in the years ahead.

This book has given you all of the tools you need to make an impact and to set you off in the right direction. The only thing you need to add is your commitment to making it work. You should be optimistic about the future – you have everything you need to make it great.

Now it's up to you.

Acknowledgements

I've been able to write this book because of the support, teaching and guidance of so many people over the last three decades.

The first thank you is to my mum. If you hadn't encouraged me to work in the box office at Wembley all those years ago, I would never have gone down the path I have. A special mention must go to Bruce Osborne. Thanks for taking a chance on a trappy teenager and giving me solid foundations to work from. You showed more belief in my ability than I had, and I'll always be grateful for that.

Thank you to all the colleagues that I have worked with over the years. Your experience and guidance helped to shape my development throughout my career. This industry is full of decent human beings, and many of

ALL TICKET

you have become good friends – not just work colleagues. A very big thank you to Ian Murphy. We've known and worked with each other since our early twenties and been through many ticketing highs and lows together. Thanks for writing the Foreword while casually managing the ticketing of a UEFA final at the same time – a class act!

A huge shout of admiration goes to everyone currently working at Kaizen. I live my dream every day, working with a bunch of dedicated and talented people. We've come so far, and the job isn't done yet. I can't wait to see what we can achieve together. A special thanks to Kieran for being the yin to my yang and masterminding the technology that keeps us ahead of the game.

If you've worked with us at any point over the past eleven years – you have my eternal gratitude. Every club has contributed to the evolution of something very special. Thank you for playing a part in making that happen.

Thank you to everyone at Rethink for helping me to put this book into the world. A big thanks in particular to Vicky for helping me organise my thoughts and teaching me a process that made writing a book therapeutic and nothing like the overwhelming task I thought it would be.

Finally, I want to show appreciation to my family. My wife Hayley and my kids, Warren, Blake and James.

ACKNOWLEDGEMENTS

Hayley – you've backed me from day one, even when times have been tough and you would have been well within your rights to tell me to give up and get a proper job. You've always pushed me to keep going. Don't underestimate how important you've been in getting us this far.

I'd love to have been able to shout everyone out personally, but that would've been another book in itself, so if you're reading this – thank you.

The Author

 David Lynam is the Founder and Managing Director of Kaizen Ticketing, where he has worked with over 130 football clubs at all levels. He wrote this book to share the proven strategies and tools that have transformed ticketing operations across the football pyramid.

Connect with David and find out more about his work:

🌐 www.kaizenticketing.com

in www.linkedin.com/in/dlynam1

f search 'All Ticket Community'